FILMMAKERS SERIES
edited by
ANTHONY SLIDE

1. *James Whale*, by James Curtis. 1982
2. *Cinema Stylists*, by John Belton. 1983
3. *Harry Langdon*, by William Schelly. 1982
4. *William A. Wellman*, by Frank Thompson. 1983
5. *Stanley Donen*, by Joseph Casper. 1983
6. *Brian De Palma*, by Michael Bliss. 1983
7. *J. Stuart Blackton*, by Marian Blackton Trimble. 1985
8. *Martin Scorsese and Michael Cimino*, by Michael Bliss. 1985
9. *Franklin J. Schaffner*, by Erwin Kim. 1985
10. *D. W. Griffith and the Biograph Company*, by Cooper C. Graham et al. 1985
11. *Some Day We'll Laugh: An Autobiography*, by Esther Ralston. 1985
12. *The Memoirs of Alice Guy Blaché*, 2nd ed., translated by Roberta and Simone Blaché. 1996
13. *Leni Riefenstahl and Olympia*, by Cooper C. Graham. 1986
14. *Robert Florey*, by Brian Taves. 1987
15. *Henry King's America*, by Walter Coppedge. 1986
16. *Aldous Huxley and Film*, by Virginia M. Clark. 1987
17. *Five American Cinematographers*, by Scott Eyman. 1987
18. *Cinematographers on the Art and Craft of Cinematography*, by Anna Kate Sterling. 1987
19. *Stars of the Silents*, by Edward Wagenknecht. 1987
20. *Twentieth Century-Fox*, by Aubrey Solomon. 1988
21. *Highlights and Shadows: The Memoirs of a Hollywood Cameraman*, by Charles G. Clarke. 1989
22. *I Went That-a-Way: The Memoirs of a Western Film Director*, by Harry L. Fraser; edited by Wheeler Winston Dixon and Audrey Brown Fraser. 1990
23. *Order in the Universe: The Films of John Carpenter*, by Robert C. Cumbow. 1990 (*out of print; see No. 70*)
24. *The Films of Freddie Francis*, by Wheeler Winston Dixon. 1991
25. *Hollywood Be Thy Name*, by William Bakewell. 1991
26. *The Charm of Evil: The Life and Films of Terence Fisher*, by Wheeler Winston Dixon. 1991
27. *Lionheart in Hollywood: The Autobiography of Henry Wilcoxon*, with Katherine Orrison. 1991

A Take on British TV Drama

Stories from the Golden Years

Christopher Neame

Filmmakers Series, No. 112

THE SCARECROW PRESS, INC.
Lanham, Maryland • Toronto • Oxford
2004

SCARECROW PRESS, INC.

Published in the United States of America
by Scarecrow Press, Inc.
A wholly owned subsidiary of The Rowman & Littlefield Publishing Group, Inc.
4501 Forbes Boulevard, Suite 200, Lanham, Maryland 20706
www.scarecrowpress.com

PO Box 317
Oxford
OX2 9RU, UK

British Library Cataloguing in Publication Information Available

Library of Congress Cataloging-in-Publication Data

A take on British tv drama : stories from the golden years / Christopher Neame.
    p. cm. — (Filmmakers series ; no. 112)
  Includes index.
  ISBN 0-8108-5012-5 (hard. : alk. paper)
  1. Television—Production and direction—Great Britain. I. Title. II. Series.
PN1992.75.N43 2004
791.4502'32—dc22

2004003959

∞™ The paper used in this publication meets the minimum requirements of
American National Standard for Information Sciences—Permanence of Paper
for Printed Library Materials, ANSI/NISO Z39.48-1992.
Manufactured in the United States of America.

~

Contents

~

Foreword

Reading Christopher Neame's book is an unusual pleasure; partly like a look at someone's diary, partly like that rarity, a Christmas catch-up letter from someone with really interesting stories to tell, and very like a dinner to remember with a wonderful and frank conversationalist—the disparate stories and adventures tied together without effort and pleasingly informing each other. Read it for a direct sense of what it is to produce for television, what it takes, what it's like to live the life, and who is best suited to the task by temperament and appetite. That will be someone who shares the author's taste for bedlam, improvisation, jury-rigged, skin-of-your-teeth escapes from disaster and the great joke and noble enterprise that is the entertainment business along with the more seriously focused aspect. Christopher's characteristic optimism, pride in the work, his *Boys' Own* can-do spirit, and his prejudices and warmth are cheerfully exposed. The telling is direct. His book is full of really useful information about how the adventurous artist may stay a step ahead of the bean counters. It is a delightful reminder of what makes him a pleasure to be around and why the "behind-the-scenes" story is regularly just as precious and valuable to those who are lucky enough to experience it as is the final result of a production for others.

Read and enjoy.

—Sam Waterston

~

Preface

"You don't want to do television productions," said my wife, Caroline, in her sometimes clipped tone one evening in March 1978.

After a moment's thought I replied, "No. I'll telephone him in the morning and say it's off."

"It" referred to a meeting called by a man named Johnny Goodman, who had suggested I might work as the associate producer on a television series for Thames Television's subsidiary, Euston Films. Johnny was an old chum from my early days at Elstree Studios and, barely a month before, had been appointed as this freethinking company's head of production. The idea was for me to discuss matters with the series' creator, John Hawkesworth, to see if we might get along together.

Even though I was unemployed at the moment, the idea of television was supposed to be beneath me, and, being the third-generation member of a film industry family, my eyes remained focused firmly on the big screen. I had recently made my debut as the producer of a feature film, at a time when it was nigh on impossible to get anything off the ground. In order to entice audiences out of the comfort of their armchairs and across the street into a cinema, one had to provide something they couldn't see on TV. In reality there were only two ways to go—produce very expensive action movies (in England?) or give the public sex on a shoestring to satisfy their voyeuristic instincts. No contest—sex it had to be, but my intention wasn't to do some sleazy picture with a double-entendre title like *The Comings and Goings of a Parking Lot Attendant*. No, I decided, as I idled away some time in the bathtub; it had to be something much more elegant—a period piece with pretty frocks (when they were worn), romantic music and settings, soft lighting. And why not have something vaguely adventurous like horse riding or, even better, a stunt flying sequence? Such scenes can be expensive to shoot, but as an aviator and an ex-member of the camera department, I knew there had to be an economical way of going about such apparent extravagance. All that was needed was a story line. By midday it was beginning to emerge—a loose reworking of a Guy de Maupassant novelette. Originally set in a wet nineteenth-century Paris, it would be relocated to southern England in the summer of 1928. I suspect 1928 was chosen because skirts were shortish then and bosoms not distastefully overwhelming.

Pencil was put to paper and some rapid writing done (I couldn't afford to hire a writer), and by the following evening the first draft of the screenplay had been rushed onto paper. The next thing was to find a director, so I approached someone with whom I had worked before. Henry Herbert had been a winner at the Chicago International Film Festival for a documentary about blind children, *What Colour Is the Wind?* He tacitly expressed interest, but before too long we became production associates for my proposed film as well as many future projects.

Right from the outset we made an unbreakable decision to give ourselves a maximum of six weeks (allowing a bit of time for filming before the summer expired) to raise the capital; if we failed, the concept would be abandoned. We didn't fail. Next, we started trawling for a young leading actress who was prepared to "perform" (in two senses of the word) in the nude—still a bit risqué then. Again we were ultimately successful. Our continued aim was to produce something of quality, and because of the slackness of the industry we were lucky enough to be in a position to engage cameraman Jack Hildyard at a very modest price. Jack had won an Oscar for his cinematography on *The Bridge on the River Kwai*. We also persuaded American poet and composer Rod McKuen to write the score and some songs. Our principal set was a country house of faded grandeur, but it suited the narrative well with its plush reds and rich greens—all set in a golden landscape.

The film did passably well at the box office until our leading lady hit the headlines and attendance suddenly rocketed. On the downside, Alan Brien, the bearded *Sunday Observer* film critic (a good one, if there are such souls) complained that Messrs. Neame and Herbert should not have been so tame with their drawing room piece; after all, censorship had started to relax, and we could have been more sexually explicit. Another critic, Kenneth Tynan, who was also a friend, saw it and was not very amused. The movie did not even get to first base in his realm of eroticism—and by now most people know all about that realm!

The movie was called *Emily*, and in the eponymous role was Koo Stark, who, if the press were to be believed, shortly embarked on an affair with Prince Andrew. It was this situation that increased the box office figures because the public wanted to see for themselves what a member of the Royal Family reportedly saw in private! All that aside, Koo was a highly professional young actress, and I have the very greatest respect for her and the dignified way in which she has continued to handle her life.

The worst reviews were for the script. This was fair enough, but, after all, it had been written in a total of seventeen hours—essentially as a vehicle for me to produce and ipso facto, defies criticism in my eyes. The only really unfair thing came about when we started printing copies of the screenplay. What name to put on the front cover? Well, I certainly didn't want mine, so I literally pulled one from the air there and then—"Anthony Morris." Many years later a real Anthony Morris emerged as a screenwriter, and on the Internet Movie Database (IMDB) it is he who bears the brunt of my rushed work. Sorry! The point is that in a highly depressed market, I had managed to emerge as a producer.

It is a shame Henry Herbert unfairly carried the "Cross of Emily" as a sex flick for a long time to come. In his other life he was the 17th Earl of Pembroke, owner of one of England's very finest estates—Wilton House, in Wiltshire—and so there was plenty of press copy along the lines of "Earl's sexy romp." You can imagine the rest. . . . Again not fair, as the tall, lean, and naturally sophisticated "H," as I called him, has a very good track record as a filmmaker.

By spring 1978, *Emily* was a year behind me, and I had to focus on the future. But as I went to bed that night in March, I was convinced that Caroline was right to be sniffy about television productions and that there could be no future involvement for me with the small screen. In the morning, however, a very different thought came to mind. The truth of the matter was the British film industry was alive and kicking—but it was living in television!

Looking back, how could I have realized then that I was standing on the brink of the most exciting and innovative decade of British television drama—the likes of which we will never know again.

~

Principal Characters
(in Order of Appearance)

Caroline Neame (later Anderson):	*My wife until 1980*
Johnny Goodman:	*Euston Films (later Central Films) head of production*
John Hawkesworth:	*Producer*
Henry Herbert:	*Director*
Hayley Mills:	*Actress*
Anthony Andrews:	*Actor*
Weston Drury Jr., "Budge":	*Casting director*
Judy Geeson:	*Actress*
Patrick Cassavetti:	*Location manager, later producer*
Malcolm Burgess:	*Production accountant, later associate producer*
Ferdinand Fairfax:	*Director*
Roy Ward Baker:	*Director*
Verity Lambert:	*Head of Thames TV drama and executive producer*
Norman Langley:	*Cinematographer*
Liz Bunton:	*Production coordinator, later producer*
Jack Rosenthal:	*Writer*

Bob Brooks:	*Director*
John Whitney:	*Executive*
Simon Olswang:	*Lawyer*
John Pringle:	*Executive*
Monty Ruben:	*Kenyan businessman and film executive*
Elspeth Huxley:	*Writer*
Holly Aird:	*Actress*
Dai Bradley:	*Actor*
Clifton Brandon:	*Production manager*
Mike Fox:	*Cameraman*
Roy Stannard:	*Set designer*
Ian Wilson:	*Cinematographer*
Sam Waterston:	*Actor*
A. C. Weary:	*Actor*
Julian Glover:	*Actor*
Sally-Ann Neame (previously Abel):	*My wife*
James Mitchell:	*Executive producer*
Peter Bowles:	*Actor*
Geoff Glover:	*Camera operator*
Peter Sykes:	*Director*
Lloyd Shirley:	*Head of Thames TV drama and executive producer*
Muir Sutherland:	*Director of programs at Thames TV*
Bryan Cowgill:	*Managing director of Thames TV*
Graham Greene:	*Novelist*
Fr. Leopoldo Durán:	*Secular priest*
Paco Lara:	*Production manager*
Yvonne Cloetta:	*Graham Greene's companion of thirty-one years*
Alec Guinness:	*Actor*
Rodney Bennett:	*Director*
Leo McKern:	*Actor*
George Roman:	*Stage director*
Michael Wearing:	*Producer*

Richard Loncraine: *Director*
Bernard Hill: *Actor*
Jean Marsh: *Actress*
Eileen Atkins: *Actress*
Edward Bennett: *Director*
Ben Chaplin: *Actor*
Ted Childs: *Managing director of Central Films*

Ann Tricklebank: *Associate producer, later producer*

David Young: *Script editor*
Anthony Garner: *Director*
Ian Mune: *Director*
Gary Love: *Actor, later director*
Jerome Flynn: *Actor*
Robson Green: *Actor*
Ethan Lewis Maltby: *Composer*

CHAPTER ONE

~

Lateral Thinking

So the meeting with Johnny Goodman and John Hawkesworth was not canceled, and we got together two days later at the Euston Films offices (a half-condemned gothic building that had been part of London's St. Paul's School, before the campus relocated). We all seemed to get on well, and they gave me a copy of the script for the first episode, the only one written by then, and told me they'd let me know if I was "on" in a couple of days. Barely twenty-four hours later, my excitement was such that I ignored the principle of "Don't call us, we'll call you" and phoned Johnny.

"I don't know whether you want me to do the series or not, but one thing I must tell you, regardless, is that the first script is absolutely bloody wonderful." It really was far and away better than anything I had ever seen on television—characters, plot, tension, atmosphere, it had it all and more.

"Funny you should call now," said Johnny. "We've just made a decision and we'd like you to do the show—if you want to. Though the money's not very good." (The money's not very good is a tried-and-tested line and usually works well enough if you're not a Hollywood star—mind you, it seems Nicole Kidman accepted a small amount to appear on stage in London.) Much later I was to learn that John

1

Hawkesworth had preferred another candidate to me, but Johnny had talked him round.

I'd first met Hawkesworth as a teenager in 1957 when he was an art director and working with my father, Ronald Neame, on a film at Pinewood Studios. John was a cheerful man with a ruddy complexion and red hair whose only real fault was his habit of smoking very pungent cigars. He claimed it was Ronnie who had taught him how to be a producer, and it seemed he was now about to do the same for me.

As a young man he had studied painting in Paris under Pablo Picasso, and then World War II swept him away to become a tank commander in the Grenadier Guards. On demobilization he had entered the film industry in the art department at Denham Studios under the aegis of Alexander Korda's brother Vincent. Soon John graduated to the senior role and designed the sets for such films as *The Third Man* and *The Fallen Idol*. He first worked with my father on *The Man Who Never Was* in 1954 and then subsequently on *Windom's Way*. Intent on becoming a writer/producer, he started off by scripting *Tiger Bay*. The film, a tense thriller involving a little girl and a killer on the run, introduced Hayley Mills to the public. It was very good indeed. But afterward, for one of those inexplicable reasons, things must have got a bit quiet for him in the cinema world, and so he turned his considerable talent into making some of the newly arrived TV commercials. Eventually breaking away from those, he wrote and produced three television series, most notably *Upstairs, Downstairs*.

By the time we remet at Euston Films, his red hair had changed to a thinning gray; however, his complexion was as ruddy as ever, and his blue eyes still effervescent.

The show we were about to embark on (thirteen episodes of one television hour each) was extremely ambitious—it was also highly dramatic. So there I was at the outset of a new branch of my career, and I couldn't wait to get on with *Danger UXB*. (Public warning signs were placed in areas where bombs had fallen on London during the blitz of World War II and failed to detonate, hence "Unexploded Bomb.")

Aside from the all-important matter of monitoring the ongoing progress of scripts, the first three things to be addressed were the size of the screen we were to work to, the use of camera lenses, and a color style consistent with London during the blitz. It is probably necessary to explain that, unlike cinema, a producer in television has an added and very crucial role that is perhaps best described as an "executive director." The schedules for episodic shows can rarely be handled by one director, whose responsibilities involve (or used to involve) scripting, casting, filming, editing, music recording, dubbing, and delivery. So with a director turnaround limited to about one show in four, it has to be the producer who remains the constant factor.

I had always been told that because the television screen was so much smaller than a theater's, one had to keep the camera in much closer to the (confined) action. This seemed reasonable enough until I got to thinking about the theory. Surely, I reasoned, it depends on how close you are to the screen. Simply by putting my thumb to my nose and stretching my fingers wide, I then angled my hand ninety degrees clockwise and counted the number of fingers it took to fill the screen of an average cinema. A three-finger width. At home I did the same thing with a television set. Simple, really: take up a reasonable position, and the relative size is not vastly different. It's obvious that the closer you get to either screen, the larger the image. Bottom-right-hand line—no concessions need be made; we would shoot a television series just like any other film.

It was the lenses that created the biggest problem. Here were two opposing points of view. Our forebears had determined that for cinematography the most perfectly composed pictures would be created on 35-mm film. Company accountants took another standpoint. The cost of 16-mm film and its processing is much cheaper than 35 mm, and the resultant product seems to be up to an acceptable standard in their ledger-accustomed eyes. Ho-hum! And another problem: at less than half the film width, shorter-focus lenses had to be used to get the equivalent acceptance angle of 35 mm—in other words, a one-inch lens would be employed in place of a two-inch. The result is "ballooning" faces in close-up—not good for pretty girls. However, the holders of stubby red pencils had the final word, and *Danger UXB* would just have to live with the less than perfect situation. It was shot on 16 mm.

Color— London unlit by night, khaki uniforms, cream sticky tape across windowpanes to give some safety from flying glass in the likely event of nearby explosions. And the bleakest of all, the air raid shelters. One John and I visited was exactly as it had been during the blitz, even down to contemporary newspapers strewn about. This was located deep below Clapham Common and was an uncompleted (because of the war) Underground station. Okay, we had to go with the drab colors, but there was another side to the coin. It is curious to note that for a lot of people living in London (and elsewhere in England and abroad), the war years were an invigorating and happy time, unwarranted death and destruction aside. There were nightclubs, dance halls, and restaurants all putting on a cheerful face, and there was passion. These would bring the moments of color to our audience just as they had brought them to the dwellers of a threatened city when they let their hair down.

Slowly Hawkesworth and I put the puzzle together. Now to cast and crew. The main protagonist is a young man seconded into the army as a bomb disposal officer. What an absolutely terrifying job—defusing an unexploded bomb. Just imagine it: unscrew the detonator . . . slowly . . . slowly . . . and then . . . tick-a, tick-a, tick-a . . . How long have you got? Get up and run? Or finish the job? Tick-a, tick-a, tick-a . . .

We saw a lot of actors for the part of "Lieutenant Brian Ash." Whoever he was to be had to portray a young man who was attractive to women without actually knowing it—softly and well spoken (women, most certainly in the middle of the twentieth century, were attracted by a voice with a hint of sophistication)—a gentle sense of humor—able to be positive when needed—and an instinctive leader, again being totally unaware of the quality within himself. Suffice it to say, the search finished the day we met Anthony Andrews. Hawkesworth had cast him in *Upstairs, Downstairs*, and I was instantly won over by him.

There were many others to be cast in supporting parts—particularly the sappers forming Ash's squad, but this wasn't hard. England has always had a vast supply of superb actors eager to work in an overcrowded profession. I suspect this talent has been harnessed by the rigorous demands of the highly commendable drama schools endemic to our country from very early times.

Not only did we have our own experience to work on but also our casting director's. Weston Drury Jr., "Budge," as we all knew him, was a big, white-bearded man who was one of the most knowledgeable people in his profession—for many years he had been in charge of casting at Rank's Pinewood Studios and had seen the likes of Dirk Bogarde and Peter Finch pass through his doors on their way to "A" or "B" Stage and onward to world stardom. Budge had lived through World War II and had worked with the young actors of the day who were now ripe to play the older people in our drama. (Budge's birth year is recorded on IMDB as 24th December 1892, which would have made him eighty-five at the time of our series. It has to be said that he looked very hearty for a man of so many years—could it have been he was Weston Drury Sr. as well?)

Now our attentions turned to "Susan Mount," a woman married too early within her scientific father's circle and who would, before long, embark on an adulterous affair with Lieutenant Ash. Wholesome, fair-haired, bright, pretty, sexy, and intelligent. Judy Geeson was a contender—I had worked with her a few years before at Hammer Films, and she came for an interview. Hawkesworth seemed to relish these occasions and at the appointed time—after a polite introductory period—he would proceed to relate to the interviewee the entire thirteen hours' worth of story. He did it very well. Judy spoke little as she listened, and when finally she said something, it was (as she admitted to me later) in a predetermined, clipped accent so evocative of the 1940s—take Celia Johnson in *Brief Encounter*. It wasn't simply the way she spoke but her whole demeanor that told us Judy was our girl.

The running order of episodes caused some consternation. The series rule, then, was that any one of the films could be televised in any order—presumably this was because as the hoped-for buildup of audience numbers kicked in, no one would lose the plot or the company could sell various sized batches to overseas TV stations unable to afford the entire show. Well it was simply impossible for us. Technically, in financial terms and programming, our production was considered to be episodic, whereas actually it was a serial. Best not to say too much—just arrange to deliver each film to the company a week before it aired so they had only one program in hand. This situation was subsequently explained away with sincerely apologetic words about our inefficiency!

What was of much greater concern were the dwindling daylight hours. During the filming of the first half of the show, there would be enough of the day to continue shooting exterior scenes until around six o'clock in the evening. But then suddenly—it always comes as a sudden shock however well one is prepared—the clocks change back to Greenwich mean time (or winter time), and filming daylight scenes outside would have to finish by five o'clock and before long by four o'clock. Nothing to be done about it but instruct the writers to create more night exterior scenes as the schedule took us ever onward to December.

This and other inevitable constraints were instructive—I began to realize how one could create a story and atmosphere because of a "needs must" situation. The times are countless when we have had to come up with an innovative idea of how to shoot a sequence with greater demands than our budget allowed—surprisingly, the outcome most often exceeded all expectations. In other words, having one's back against the wall makes for greater creativity. (There are several examples to illustrate this, but few could beat the extraordinary method of filming a nineteenth-century merchantman running onto rocks for *The Irish RM*—but that lay a few years ahead.)

It was fascinating to learn about characters (how to invent them and how to write them) and who they are, what they are—their likes, their dislikes—essentially what makes them individuals. Then the question of whether we have empathy for them or despise them. The rule had to be that if you didn't care one way or the other, they were out of the story from the start. Hawkesworth took control of this brilliantly. Each person we were to encounter on screen would hold our attention, and, at the risk of using a tired expression, we could laugh and cry with him or her. I think the boldest thing he proposed was the sudden death of a character we would get to admire during the first four films. Suddenly he is blown up!

"John," I said, "We can't wipe out someone we've been attached to so soon on in the series."

"Oh, I think we can."

And of course he was so right. After the episode aired, the audience figures shot up.

What was happening to me, under John's sure tutelage, was a gentle induction into storytelling. Let's be honest, cinema and television are only more sophisticated extensions of an earlier form of expression—a means of conveying incidents from one person to another. Excitement, laughter, horror, fear, eroticism, panic, or whatever are the emotions filmmakers (and as, I was now discovering, television producers) are both entitled and obliged to exploit.

As the story covered some three years, we needed to have a variety of different bombs to show the technological advancement of air attack. They would be fiberglass replicas, if for no other reason than to avoid the risk of our prop men going off sick with hernias. And they had to be correct in every detail. Coming most willingly to our aid were the officers of the Royal Engineers, based near Rochester in Kent. (An interesting aside is the badge they still proudly wear on their uniform sleeves—it was designed by the wartime matriarch of the Royal Family, Queen Mary, grandmother of Queen Elizabeth.) The Royal Engineers have a private museum housing every type of weapon, and they gave us permission to re-create their samples. The museum is fascinating—the pretty little yellow butterfly bomb that landed delicately on drogues and waited for some curious child to pick it up as a toy—the Herman, a very, very large and powerful bomb—those in between—and then the V1 or Doodlebug, a pilotless weapon targeted at London. (A little later in the war came the most devastating device of them all—Wernher von Braun's V2, the prototype of the modern intercontinental ballistic missiles and, on a cheerier note, space travel.)

My first and subsequent visits to this museum were enthralling, although frightening, and I determined from the outset to take as many people involved in the production as possible to see the exhibits so they could properly understand what the heartbeat of the show was all about. Now here's a funny thing—but I must be careful (I am no budding Freud—everyone reacted in exactly the same way. They all had to touch the bombs. More often than not, a surreptitious hand would reach out, and the women, in particular, would appear to stroke the surface gently as if receiving some sort of power from these infernal devices. Perhaps phallic—who knows? Nevertheless, invariably the moment became stilled by some inexplicable frisson.

It was the thrill of this devastating power within the bombs that gave *Danger UXB* its most obvious hardware edge—but for thirteen episodes? Could we ever sustain it? Yes. We had engaging characters, we had love and raw sex, we had the imminent threat of instant death, and we had comedy—the natural comedy of very real situations in an utterly explosive world. Consider it in the simplest of terms—how many ways can you cook an egg? (Nevertheless, thank God, we didn't have to make a second batch of thirteen episodes! Although I daresay we could have done so had Thames Television realized it had a major success on its hands and commissioned more—an example of where the production of British TV series differed from the U.S. method, which was, and is, to squeeze the last drop of juice from them.)

Initially there were director snags—many "possibles" sprang to mind, but they were of the world of cinema, and few had yet taken a serious look at television. This was a disappointment, as we wanted to give the show a feature film quality. There was one man, though, who had an excellent track record for work on the small screen. We met him, liked him, and engaged him to direct the opening episode, so at least we were on our way.

Danger UXB was to be a location production—no studio work—and our base was a disused school in Clapham, southwest London. It was perfect because during the war many bomb disposal units operated out of such buildings; consequently, it would also be wonderful, for loads of interior scenes and certain constructed sets, like nightclubs and front parlors (even a sewer), could go up in the old gymnasium. Location exteriors would be found as nearby as possible for schedule and budgetary reasons. Patrick Cassavetti, now a well-regarded producer (whose credits include the notable *Mona Lisa*), was in charge of locations, but the poor chap could not find anything worthwhile within the normal parameters of two or three miles and was becoming desperate as we neared the principal photography date.

"Then we'll just have to bite the bullet and go further afield," I reassured him.

The puzzle he had to contend with was a combination of modern urbanization—yellow lines, parking meters, the constant to-ing and fro-ing of traffic, parking restrictions for equipment vehicles, the noise of cars (we could afford little rerecording time for dialogue), aircraft on their way in or out of Heathrow, and more besides. The following weekend we went together on a wider search and came up with several possibilities. Though what about the cars outside their owners' homes?

Patrick could put a note through mailboxes in residential streets explaining what we were planning—and most people are cooperative under the circumstances—however, if someone was away for a month, we'd still be left with a "rogue" 1970s car in a 1940s setting, and it would be illegal to move it (one car maybe, just once, though we didn't want to get the reputation of certain "cavalier" directors who had total disregard for the property of others!). So we came up with one of those needs-must ideas to overcome the impossible. Andersen Shelters. These were reinforced structures hastily erected as a protection from the falling bombs, and, as luck would have it, they were frequently placed in the curbside. A lightweight structure of our own could be put around a visually unwanted car (should you ever see UXB, imagine a red Ford hidden behind a couple of flimsy portable walls). Another idea was created over the weekend—two-dimensional sandbags. Banks of sandbags of various sizes could be seen throughout southern England during the war, and all we needed was a painted scenery flat positioned as required to disguise the inappropriate. These devices saved our day. (Here I must record the special ingenuity of one of the later directors who had the perfect London location apart from a modern three-foot-high traffic direction sign on an island in the center of the road—he overcame this "eyesore" by having two sailors standing there with one of their canvas bags pulled down over it, as if placed on the ground for a moment while they chatted.)

On the Tuesday of the following week, John Hawkesworth bustled into our shared office at around 5:00 P.M.—his face far ruddier than usual and the tip of his pungent cigar glowing white hot.

"What's the matter?" I asked.

Huff-puff as he gathered up the contents of his briefcase and left.

"John?"

Huff-puff from the doorway as he scurried out.

The next morning I again asked him what it had all been about.

He was still angry. "Fucking director!"

John was not averse to so-called fruity language—infrequently used, appropriately used, but only this once, during our long association, used so vehemently. He, the first director designate, and Patrick Cassavetti had visited various location sites, and, because they were more than three miles distant from our base, the director had refused to get out of the car and even look at them. I think he resigned the same day, which was just as well—except it left us precariously close to starting with no one at the camera's helm.

Then our production accountant, Malcolm Burgess, came up with a name. Ferdinand Fairfax, who I had already met on social occasions, was just breaking into drama from documentaries, and he made a good impression when we interviewed him. All we needed to do was get "approval" from our executive producer, Verity Lambert, at Thames Television to hire him. She went along with our wishes, and Ferdy was on his way to a first-rate career that would take him all the way around the world. My suggestion for another director was not as well received. Roy Ward Baker has had a notable career stretching back over many decades; his cinema films include *Morning Departure*, *The One That Got Away*, and *A Night to Remember*—the only highly memorable movie about the *Titanic* disaster. We had worked together when I was an assistant director on two Hammer films—*Quatermass and the Pit* and *The Anniversary* starring Bette Davis. More recently he had turned his hand to television, directing episodes of *The Saint*, with Roger Moore, and *The Avengers*, with Patrick Macnee, to name just two. The only trouble was Roy had a reputation for irascibility. This was not fair—he was simply a perfectionist and could not tolerate incompetence or carelessness of any kind. I speak with some authority about this because we have, over the years, done many productions together, and I have always found him to be utterly charming. There was nothing for it but to "stay on the case" and win Verity round. She finally consented to Roy's engagement with the cautionary words, "Be it on your own heads." It is good to report that she was to go on to use Roy on a later production—*Minder*.

It was just past midsummer's day when we started shooting, with Ferdy in the hot seat. The very opening sequence was of an unidentified officer attempting to defuse the latest German weapon—it was always the officers' duty:

INT. SHAFT. DAY.
The camera moves down to a close shot of the young man as he unscrews the detonator from the side of the bomb . . .

Suddenly he hears an unfamiliar sound . . . Stops . . .
Ticking . . .
He listens, knowing what it must mean . . .
The camera closes in more . . .
He starts unscrewing the fuse again . . .
WHOOMPH . . .
EXT. LONDON'S EAST END. DAY.
A pall of smoke billows into the sky . . .
(This is written from memory and was not as scripted word for word
   by John Hawkesworth.)

When edited, the dramatic effect was all right but not good enough. It
worked simply like this: the camera moving down the shaft, the warning *ticks*, four frames of clear celluloid to create a flash on screen, and
then a long shot of the pyre going upward. Cognizant of David Lean's
shocking cut when the convict Magwitch is first seen in *Great Expectations*, I knew we could, somehow or other, make our explosion much
more powerful. All the visuals were perfect, so the improvement would
have to be to the sound track. Logically, the sound editors had placed
the very start of the blast a fraction of a second after the flash (to be exact, a twenty-fifth of a second). We tried delaying it by up to four picture frames—around a sixth of a second. No, it wasn't working. Let's go
the other way—place the *Whoomph* ahead of the screen flash. One
frame, two frames, three frames, and something was starting to happen—
one more frame in advance and the screen exploded! During the opening moments of a showing of this film at BAFTA's West End theater,
the invited audience of around a hundred leapt out of their seats in
surprise—including my father, who was sitting beside me.

By the end of the first week of shooting, we had slipped an unacceptable half a day behind schedule. No one was to blame, but it was
essential to talk over the situation with Ferdy. One thing had to be
made clear—each episode would be allowed its ten-day schedule of
principal photography over two weeks and no more. On every other
Monday, a new episode had to start filming, come what may. If there
was any drifting, a director would be given a small crew and the use of
actors, when available, to mop up. (On one occasion to come, there

were two directors shooting at either end of the same corridor and each complaining that the other was in the way! All I could do was laugh and tell them both it had taken me years to organize such discombobulation.) Ferdy, who has a smiling "What You See Is What You Get" face, was very responsive and understood our determination to stay on course. From then on, if he were running out of time, he would leave aside a small amount of work that could be facilitated later on. What this boiled down to was working together, which seems to be a bit of a thing of the past!

A potential cause of delay was London's low overhead aircraft—about one every three minutes on the landing path to Heathrow—the sound of their engines caused a particular problem when two shots were cut together, one with the noise on the sound track and one without. This difficulty was overcome by the introduction of our "Duty Dakota." These wonderful aircraft were frequently heard overhead during the war, so we found a recording of one coming up from the distance, passing above, and fading away into the distance again. By incorporating it in the final sound mix, with the throaty engines thrumming at their maximum to coincide with the offending Boeing, no one was aware of the jet.

A terrible accident happened when we were halfway through episode 1—and Tony Andrew's wife was in a critical condition. Georgina Simpson, heiress to her father's famous store on Piccadilly, had taken a fall at a horse show. Tony was torn between two loyalties—his wife and our production. Unquestionably, Georgina came first (and from the production's standpoint we were insured against such calamities), but she was in a coma, and there was little he could do. Consequently, to try and take his mind off the tragedy, he decided to carry on with filming. Each evening he would be released as early as possible to be at her bedside, silently remain with her until midnight or so, snatch a few hours sleep, be at the hospital at daybreak, and then come on to work by 8 A.M. Happily, Georgina regained consciousness after three days, but the whole horrible experience had taken its toll on Tony. He looked terrible to the extent that it would have been impossible to continue shooting on him, except for one thing. The sequence being covered at the time was Lieutenant Ash's first experience with an unexploded bomb. Invariably, every Royal Engineer officer looked ghastly while undergoing such a procedure. Tony and I were able to laugh about it afterward.

As photography continued, more and more scripts were being completed, and a variety of directors came in for preproduction—including the casting of episodic parts with Budge Drury. One of these directors was my good pal Henry Herbert. A tall and lean man of inbred aristocratic mien, he had a delightfully schoolboyish sense of humor and managed to wear two hats without effort. On set, all and sundry called him Henry or "Guv" or whatever, but when he was at his lovely Wilton House, it was "My Lord." In both situations, there were no airs and graces about him, and he could slip from one role to the other seamlessly. He was a man with the most generous of hearts. John Hawkesworth took to him immediately—subsequently asking him to direct an excellent retelling of the Oscar Wilde story, starring Sir Michael Gambon. It was made by a company of which both Hawkesworth and I were partners (although *Forbidden Passion: Oscar Wilde* was a project in which I was not actively involved).

One of the greatest pleasures to me on *UXB* was when Tony Andrews and Judy Geeson came to me and asked if Henry could direct them in the last and most complex episode of the show. He did.

Almost every day, something connected to the history we were dealing with was unearthed, and I mean just that. Some warehouses by the River Thames were supposed to be burning out after a night air raid by bombers, and smoke canisters were placed all around and inside the building to be ignited on cue. We had advised the local fire brigade of our activity, but apparently they had to come out to a site every time a member of the public reported evidence of a fire, so they appeared during or shortly after every one of our camera setups. They were extremely good-natured about their wasted attendances and laughed along with us—until they received a genuine emergency call. A real UXB had been discovered on the other side of the river, and they shot off to cover the defusing. Extraordinary to think that more than thirty years had passed since the end of hostilities and "live" bombs were still being discovered. What is more astonishing is they are still being found today.

Four episodes "in the can," and we were beginning to feel our feet, although still remaining uncocky—and both the ever-smiling Johnny

Goodman, at Euston, with his endless stream of witty Jewish jokes, and Verity, at Thames, remained entirely supportive—they knew we were making a first-class series (serial?). If the truth be told, so did we, not an unusual feeling when working with perfect scripts. Then a bit of a sticky situation occurred.

With Ferdy Fairfax, Roy Baker, and Henry Herbert having come up trumps, we decided to take a different approach and appoint a young director straight from live television. It didn't work out, and after four days we were a good day and a half behind schedule. To be absolutely fair, he was given a particularly tough show with a location at a country house, miles off our beaten track and at least an hour away from base. But also, and much more importantly, the story line dealt with the beginnings of Susan (Judy Geeson) and Lieutenant Ash's affair. I think it was this he struggled with, not for any immature reason but simply because he had not fully taken on board the complexities of what had gone before in the narrative. Furthermore, he strived for originality of style and was perhaps overambitious for someone inexperienced in filmmaking. It couldn't go on as it was, and so, on the Friday evening of his first week, he was taken aside and told he was to be released. For anyone, this is nothing short of devastating, and he went with our greatest sympathy—thankfully to move on to a successful future.

The decision left us without a director.

"Roy, it's me," I said over the telephone to Ward Baker. "Complications and I need you to save the situation."

Hawkesworth and I met him for lunch the next day (a Greek restaurant, as I recall) and told him about our problem. Ever the professional, he agreed to step into the breach, subject to one condition—putting him up at a nearby hotel as his home was around forty miles outside London. Agreed, and cheap at half the price.

On the Monday morning, those of the crew who had not been advised of what was happening in advance looked a trifle bemused as he walked onto the set with a shooting stick in one hand and a copy of the *Times* in another. Taking immediate charge of affairs, he gave instructions for a camera track to be laid from here to there—the shooting stick used as an indicator. And while the setup was being prepared, he turned his attention to the cryptic crossword. The two points, he subsequently told me, were done intentionally to demonstrate confident and laid-back leadership. He further claims that he completed the crossword before shooting commenced—I cannot vouch for this.

Although absolute calamity had been averted, the schedule was now adrift by some two and a half days. There was, however, a way around it. A long sequence confined to one room required only Tony Andrews and Judy, and, as there was work to be done elsewhere without them, a small second unit could be employed. Director? Well, to cut a long story short, it was me.

The pair arrives at a private hotel on the edge of South London at the start of their affair. A small bedroom—lit mainly by the glow of a gas fire. Their dialogue was minimal and wonderful to play and direct. The inconsequentiality of it was what gave the scene power—the underlying sexual tension between the characters. Writing like this requires a lot of know-how, and Jeremy Paul (with whom I had been at school) did a fantastic job.

The last section to be shot was after they have made love. Tony was lying on his back while Judy, sleeping peacefully, was more or less face down in his arms with just the side of her right breast revealed. What I asked Tony to do was to run his fingers ever so gently down her naked back to her waist, and, as he stroked them back up again, the camera would crane up. Fade out for the end of "part 1."

Everything was ready, and the actors were in position. Then I noticed something wasn't quite right.

"Judy, the position of your breast makes it look a bit square. Try moving a little."

She did. "How's that?"

"Hummm—worse if anything. Try again."

"How about now?"

"Back to where it was in the first place."

She made one more attempt, and it still wasn't right.

As I said, "Judy, it might be best for me to shape it," she said, "Why don't you position it the way you want?"

She raised herself up, and I gently slipped my hand under her breast and got it to look right. Then I laughed.

"What's so funny?"

"I was just thinking what I'd tell my children if they asked what I did at work today."

Judy laughed, Tony laughed, and so did all of our small unit. It was five minutes before we were able to take the job seriously again.

It was made clear to all the writers that they should not concern themselves with the technical matters we might have to overcome—these were for us to worry about and should not get in the way of creativity. But we were nearly hoist by our own petard with one script.

A London street, seen at the beginning of the story as it had always been. People going about life, the odd car, a bicyclist here or there. Then suddenly a bomb explodes, and the street is turned into a smoking pile of rubble. How the hell could it be achieved? After a thorough search, good old Patrick Cassavetti came up with the solution. Only a few miles away, a whole area was being cleared of Victorian houses to make way for modern developments. The timing was perfect, and the demolition gang could not have been more sporting. One street was razed, and next to it was another with exactly the same type of houses as yet untouched.

A few hours in the morning filming the intact street scenes and, by early afternoon, over to the "blitzed" one. It couldn't have been simpler. But how to do the actual bomb blast? In the end, even simpler still. A fairly close shot, taken from outside, with someone's face looking through a window, and reflected in the panes of glass the fireball of a massive explosion. (It was actually a superimposed image.)

The power of the bombs could never be overstated, and for one sequence the Royal Engineers came along and detonated something pretty big on some wasteland near the River Thames. Quite horrific—the earth for many hundreds of yards rippled like rapid waves on the sea.

A series dealing with bombs would be incomplete without a sewer sequence, and, after all, John Hawkesworth had designed and built the sewers for *The Third Man*. When he saw our rushes for that section, he told me he thought it looked equally as good as his had. It was thanks to the darkly bearded Patrick, yet again, and art director, Jimmy Weatherup. The former's contribution was to find a very large storm drain that we would be allowed to film in under certain conditions—only handheld lights could be used, and one camera and a maximum number of four people were allowed down. Those four could not have been more game—Tony Andrews; Maurice Roëves, who played Lieutenant Ash's sergeant; cameraman Norman Langley; and one electrician. All were ordered to get out instantly if told to do so—a flash-flood scare! A quartz halogen lamp was held around a bend about fifty yards away to backlight the dripping brick walls, and Norman held another to illuminate the faces of the actors as they came up and past the camera.

Meanwhile, Jimmy had erected a thirty-foot length of fiberglass sewer in the gymnasium at our school base, which was where the main action took place.

Adding to the verisimilitude was Maurice's heavy bout of flu! He insisted on carrying on with his work even though he was sweating profusely. Anyone close by a bomb while it's being defused is liable to sweat profusely.

Having Norman Langley on the series was one of the biggest bonuses of all. He really is a most innovative cinematographer. Faced with one scene to film in the enormous caverns of a power station—unwilling host to a bomb—he came up with a way of photographing a very wide shot without the use of hundreds of (expensive) lights.

Lieutenant Ash enters the building in a comparatively confined angle and looks up and around . . . Cut back to the long shot for three or four seconds, so as to "sell" the location, and back in closer again with Ash walking forward for the core of the scene. In the long shot there is no movement, and the camera could be run at five picture frames per second. This gave each frame enough time to be exposed correctly from the limited daylight offered through grimy windows.

We were to present him with a similar but an even tougher challenge on *Monsignor Quixote*, which we made in Spain some years on in 1985 . . .

As the filming of *Danger UXB* continued into the depths of winter, the postproduction was in full swing, with, as usual, a deadline for the start of transmission looming. Among other elements in hand was music recording. Simon Park composed the score, and his first instruction was to write something huge for the generic opening title sequence—preferably nothing less powerful than Gustav Holst's "Mars." He didn't let us down, and we had an orchestra of about eighty members to play the section. Imagine that happening nowadays with sophisticated keyboards readily available. Composers have become the entire orchestra, but I'm afraid it just doesn't sound as good as the real instruments. What a pity the Musicians' Union became so greedy—why hadn't they learned from the plight of British dockers?

How daunting it must have been to write music for thirteen individual episodes and be given about a week each to do so and a few short hours to record.

All too soon, the six months of principal photography on *Danger UXB* was over and only half a day behind schedule. Then, after a spectacular wrap-cum-Christmas party—a memorable occasion full of laughter and pride and tears of farewell—almost everyone started going their own way—or tried to.

A few of us remained on at our Clapham base for nearly three months to complete editing and dispatching the films (in serial order) to Thames Television. But here's an odd thing about human nature and its craving for companionship—not a day went by without one, two, four, or even six of our team, cast and crew alike, returning to the base for a social get-together. Genuinely we were like a great big happy family.

Among those who stayed behind were two people who were becoming very important to me, Malcolm Burgess, the accountant (a man without the narrow-mindedness of some), who on subsequent productions would be an associate producer, and Liz Bunton, John's and my P.A. Meanwhile, old chum Johnny Goodman had become a firm and loyal friend.

With the pressure of work easing off a little, Hawkesworth and I, having decided we would like to work together again, started to consider what we might do next. Four subjects had appeal. The first was a miniseries based on H. E. Bates's novel *Fair Stood the Wind for France*, for London Weekend Television. They had the scripts, and they turned out to be very bad in our view. So that was that. The second, a novel by Ernest Raymond, titled *We, the Accused*, was soon out of the frame, as someone else had already secured the rights. Third was *The Feast of July*, another Bates story. And finally *The Flame Trees of Thika*, Elspeth Huxley's vivid portrayal of her pre–World War I upbringing in Kenya. A wonderful location for a camera—and much, much more besides. I told my wife, Caroline, how Africa has a sense of magic that almost touches one.

We pitched the latter two to Verity Lambert, inwardly believing she would opt for the Bates story, as it was set in England and was bound to be less complicated to produce, cheaper, and not as commercially risky as a period piece in Africa—although, as some wag suggested, there was always Windsor Wildlife Safari Park and its lions, a bare twenty miles from London. But what about no sun or a low sun?

Verity said she would take a look at both and get back to us before long.

UXB started airing in the United Kingdom in January 1979, with a repeat showing in the same week, and episode 11 had already been transmitted by the time I was at last able to take a break. Where better to go than a health farm for a week? What made this self-inflicted hell tenable was Tony Andrews coming along with me. While we were there, the penultimate episode went out. One sequence (taken like many from a true event) shows Lieutenant Ash defusing a bomb at the end of a pier. Suddenly the bomb goes off and violently hurls him back into the sea. Well, of course, all our co-inmates at the health farm wanted to know whether Ash had survived. We refused to tell them; they would have to wait another week to find out.

Postscript

The series was highly thought of in both the United Kingdom and the United States (in 1981). I was in Los Angeles when Masterpiece Theatre and Mobil launched the show at the ABC Center at Century City. Tony and Judy were there too—and we were able to reminisce about so many mostly very happy situations.

One of the journalists present asked me why British television drama was so slow—couldn't we speed everything up a bit? I explained how we took care to develop the characters, and, if not done properly, they would end up as two-dimensional, like too many characters in American shows. That kept him quiet, although my intention was not to be rude. A contributory factor on the slowness front is technical. For U.K. television, the film runs at twenty-five pictures per second (both in the camera and on a telecine machine), whereas in the States it is twenty-four. So at the end of the day, our fifty-minute episode plays for fifty-two minutes on Masterpiece Theatre.

Alistair Cook introduced each film to the American audience in his inimitable way—explaining the background of what London was about in those catastrophic days. He did us proud—and the series is still remembered fondly in that big wide country.

Looking at the work again, as I write this, there is only one serious flaw—the picture quality of 16-mm film in the 1970s is no longer acceptable. Had the company accountants not had their way and the larger format used, all thirteen episodes would undoubtedly still be playing somewhere around the world (subject to sensible negotiations being held with Equity about repeat fees).

As I said at the beginning, these were the early days of an extraordinary period when film and television drama united and the very best of material was emerging from British talent and going to the global market.

CHAPTER TWO

~

A Farm in Africa

INT. KNOWLEDGE BOYS' CAFE. DAY (LONDON)
One or two KNOWLEDGE BOYS sitting about with cups of tea. They seem nervous, edgy. At another table is GORDON, nonchalantly sitting back, reading a newspaper, whistling to himself. At another table is TED—the A-to-Z and list of detailed runs in front of him. He's doing last-minute revisions. TITANIC is collecting a cup of tea at the counter. He's very strained and nervous. He wanders to Ted's table.
TITANIC: Anyone sitting here? Sort of, you know. Here. And that.
TED: Help yourself.
(TITANIC sits down. Looks at the lists of runs, at the table, then at TED.)
TITANIC: *(Uncertainly)* I met you, didn't I, at the . . .
TED: Margolies. Clapham.
TITANIC: That's it! I'm Mr.—
TED: Walters. Kennington Oval.
TITANIC: *(Delighted)* That's it!
(A pause. He sips his tea. TED resumes his swotting. TITANIC racks his brain for an excuse to continue the rare treat of having an actual conversation with someone.)
Got a better memory than me, mate. I'll give you that—*free* of charge. No one ever remembers *my* name.

TED: (*Shrugs, smiles.*) Photographic, they say. Well, I say "they."
   The wife does.

TITANIC: What—for a living or what?

TED: (*Puzzled*) What?

TITANIC: 'S a good trade, by all accounts. Seasonal I should think.

TED: What is?

TITANIC: Eh?

(*TED cottons on to the misunderstanding.*)

TED: Oh, I see what you—no, no . . . I'm a Hoffman presser by trade.
   In a laundry.

TITANIC: (*Totally puzzled*) How d'you mean?

TED: No—it's all right.

TITANIC: The photographic's just a hobby, then, is that it?

TED: Yeah.

(*He returns to his swotting hastily. A pause.*)

TITANIC: I enjoyed that discussion. Don't often get the chance of
   a good discussion. Swapping points of view, pros and cons and
   that . . .

TED: (*A little warily*) No.

The above (reprinted with the permission of the author Jack Rosenthal
and the publishers Faber and Faber Ltd.) comes from Jack's script for
The Knowledge, one of two television movies I was lucky enough to produce from his work. This wonderful exchange remains an all-time favorite moment in any film I have made. ("Titanic," in case you are
wondering, was what this character's wife called him because she considered him a disaster!)

Bob Brooks, a New Yorker, was glancing at *The New Yorker* in some
reception area of a building in New York when he came across an article about "The Knowledge." The Knowledge is something special to
London—given birth by none other than Oliver Cromwell
(1599–1658), Lord Protector of England and the man responsible for
the beheading of King Charles I. It was (and still is) an exam designed
for would-be transporters of the public—later cabriolet drivers, or cabbies. Before being given a license to ply the streets, each of them has to
know the exact location of every building on every street. Not such a
big deal in the seventeenth century but an awesome task in modern

times. The whole procedure is very tough and can take three to five years to complete—and many entrants fail to run the full term. Those who succeed provide London with a unique taxi service, unlike in New York, where it is not uncommon to hail a cab, only to discover that the driver arrived from Puerto Rico the day before.

The safety standard of the driving in London is extremely high, and one can be confident about a cabbie taking an unaccompanied thirteen-year-old girl safely across the city. Also, contrary to the belief of many, there is no overcharging. Very often a longer route is used because it is quicker, and the sooner a passenger reaches his destination, the more money the cabbie will make.

The Knowledge is run by a monitoring branch of the Metropolitan Police at the London Carriage Office, where each candidate has to learn and recite verbatim the names of the roads from start to finish of thousands of different journeys. One of the most famous examiners there was a Mr. Finlay, who was known to be extremely tough and would pull any trick, however ludicrous, to put a candidate off his or her stride—this might extend to sticking pencils up his nose. The logic behind it was that they had to learn never to become flustered while carrying a passenger, however odd or awkward the person may be.

By the time Bob Brooks had finished *The New Yorker* article, the kernel of a movie was there.

Bob, a resident of England, was an excitable and physically agile, shortish, man. The co-owner of a prominent TV commercials company, he was recognized as having great creative flair in this field. Now he planned to branch out into feature-length drama. His first port of call was to meet with Jack Rosenthal and pitch the idea of *The Knowledge* to him. Jack bit.

The delightful Jack has a wonderful wit, and, being Jewish, he has the natural ability to laugh at himself. Furthermore, all his characters are invariably fully rounded, and his construction is always rock solid from beginning to end—never a word too many, never a word out of place. He has the built-in wherewithal to pull an audience's emotions in any direction he (or perhaps his characters) chooses. Jack's numerous achievements include *Bar Mitzvah Boy*, *P'tang Yang Kipperbang*, and *Yentl*.

After thoroughly researching the project, work started on the screenplay, and on completion it was shown to Verity Lambert at Euston Films.

Meanwhile, Verity had, surprisingly, opted to "green-light" *The Flame Trees of Thika*, and John Hawkesworth was commissioned to write six or eight (his choice of number) television hour-long screenplays—an assignment that would take him some four to five months. That left me on the shelf—or would have done had Verity and Johnny Goodman not asked me to produce *The Knowledge*.

I saw it as a challenge. Brooks had the reputation of being a somewhat intolerant soul—always demanding the best—and Rosenthal one of precision—ever watchful that the work of his imagination was carried out with the greatest care. Good these were the things I relished. But—there's always a "but"—we had around £100,000 (meaning twenty days of filming) to produce a masterpiece.

Everyone was astonished when I called for an extensive preparation period—ten weeks of checking every nut and bolt so that when principal photography started, nothing could or should go wrong. Preparation time is extraordinarily cheap—Bob, Jack, and I were on fixed fees, and we simply needed a couple of offices and a staff of no more than four initially.

During this period, other exciting things were happening. Hawkesworth delivered the first script for *Flame Trees*, and it captured beautifully the essence of East Africa. I had filmed there in the 1960s and had come to learn the flavor of what this was all about—a beautiful country with noble warriors, remittance men, murder stories and intrigue, and wife swapping as par for the course.

Then John Whitney stepped into my life—actually that's not quite true, John Hawkesworth simply introduced us. Whitney had been a partner with JH on *Upstairs, Downstairs* although not actively involved in the production. When I met him, he was the managing director of London's newly launched Capital Radio. The idea was for the three of us to form an independent television production company to produce *Flame Trees* for Euston/Thames—the broadcasting cartel of the major stations was about to be broken down. I brought a fourth person into what we called Blue Posts Productions (named after an old Kenyan hotel), a lawyer with a firm with a classical name for such a profession—Brecher & Co. (nearly as good as another law firm I had heard of called Argue & Phibbs). What allured me to Simon Olswang was that he had been an incredibly tough negotiator on the opposite side of the table on an earlier occasion, and I thought it wisest to have him on our side for future projects.

And then Whitney brought in John Pringle, whose pedigree was outstanding. As a young man, he had been an equerry to the Duke of Windsor (the abdicated King Edward VIII) and later, among other things, founded and ran a string of successful wine bars in New York. The Pringle family is one of the foremost in Jamaica, and when I met him, he was his country's ambassador to the Court of St. James's. Before long, John was to rename the company Consolidated Productions, and it was to go on as a thriving organization for the next ten years or so—then suddenly it imploded.

Shooting on *The Knowledge* got under way in the height of summer. And everything went strictly according to plan. One extremely clever idea from Bob Brooks was to shoot the whole film on the recently introduced Steadicam. Normally, the operator was strapped into this rather cumbersome looking device and, with the camera mounted on it, could walk about freely—all the bumps from his movement being ironed out by the device. It's heavy, though, and someone can use it for only a limited amount of time before needing a break. What we did was to mount it on a standard camera dolly and not bother about time-consuming track laying. As a result, the film has a fluidity about it, without the camera being self-conscious, which would not otherwise have been possible on our short schedule.

To hold a reader's attention, let alone the author's, one needs a conflicting situation to a greater or lesser extent; however, I am at a loss for the appropriate words when it comes to *The Knowledge*. Nothing to report. Just a comment on some of the fine cast. The disparate group of would-be cabbies were under the authority of the focal character based on Mr. Finlay at the London Carriage Office. He was played by Nigel Hawthorne (*The Madness of King George*), who gave the role a fine mixture of the draconian and near farce, a combination that created an entirely convincing, outrageous character. Two others: Ted Margolies and "Titanic" from the scene of confusion reproduced above. Ted's family had all been cabbies, and so he decided to give up his job as a Hoffman presser at the laundry and become a driver himself. He quickly memorizes all the streets of London and passes the exam in record time. His costudents take him out to celebrate, but, apart from an egg flip at

Christmas, he doesn't normally drink at all. So after having one forced on him by his friends, he gets a bit drunk and heads unsteadily for home on his moped. The police stop him, and he loses his driving licence. He learned the Knowledge for nothing! Ted was played by Jonathan Lynn, who was to go on to write two brilliant series, *Yes, Minister* and *Yes, Prime Minister*, both starring (surprise!) Nigel Hawthorne. And Titanic was portrayed by the dry-witted but underused David Ryall.

"I'm sorry, but I don't get any sense of magic about the place," said Caroline on the morning we arrived in Nairobi.

"It's something that creeps up on you, sort of suffuses through you," I responded. "But maybe you never will feel it—not everyone does."

It was November 1979, and we were on our first recce in Kenya, dosed up with malaria pills, yellow fever shots, TAB, and cholera shots (I understand the latter is a bit pointless, as there are many different strains of cholera, and if you are protected against one, it doesn't mean you're not going to suffer from another). Now we were shortly to start a safari. Just to think, we were being paid a fee to be there, with all our expenses covered, and off on a trip that tourists pay thousands of dollars to make. Our team consisted of Hawkesworth, Malcolm Burgess, our accountant, and me—and coming along with us (at our own expense) were our wives. John's wife had been known as "Pussy" since childhood, but I know of only one embarrassing incident in connection with the appellation. They had gone to a theater to see Australian comedian Barry Humphries (aka Dame Edna Everidge). Part of his act was to talk with some of the audience, starting out by asking their name. He kept the night's entire performance going with the obvious equivoque.

Nairobi was still lovely, although it had lost some of its grandness since I had last been there fifteen years earlier—just three weeks after *Uhuru* (independence from Britain). Everything was still in good repair then; there were excellent hotels and restaurants, and the main two-way road was dressed in the middle with masses of brightly colored flowers. And bougainvillea, with its vivid mauve flowers, grew wildly all over the place. What's more, if you were lucky, you might even see a lion wandering about in the city center. But by the late 1970s, it was starting to become a little run-down.

Leading our small group into "the wild" would be one of the world's truly fascinating men, Monty Ruben. His father had left Russia in the early part of the twentieth century to make a new home on the equator. So Monty is a Kenyan by birth and very much by choice. Everyone in the country seemed to know him, and his office was a center point for the film industry in Africa. Jimmy Stewart and his wife Gloria dropped by several times while we were there (Monty was a godfather to one of their daughters); Bill Holden and Stephanie Powers were frequent visitors, as were Candice Bergen, Shirley MacLaine, and just about anyone who made a film there—and many who didn't.

His introduction to movies was through his father's transport company, which put him in charge of a host of animals being sent to Los Angeles to appear in Howard Hawks's 1962 film *Hatari*. It may be apocryphal, but I have heard it told that Monty could be seen driving around the Paramount lot with a load of wild animals running behind as they took their daily exercise.

One more comment about him for the time being. Back in England, a couple of years later, I was in a brasserie in the southwest London suburb of Barnes and was telling the person with me how his daughters maintained that Monty could go into any restaurant in the world and know someone dining there.

My jaw dropped. "Good God!"

"What is it?"

"You're not going to believe this. Monty Ruben has just walked in!"

This story is not apocryphal.

There are two principal ways to go about location surveying in a country like Kenya. The most obvious is by air, or it could be done by road. The snag is that right out in the bush, the roads are mainly little more than tracks coated with a fine dust that gets into everything—one's body and one's belongings, however tightly they are sealed. During the rains, other roads can become impassable because of "black cotton"—even a four-wheel-drive vehicle is prone to slide helplessly out of control on this thick greaselike mud. But in spite of it, the only way to be thorough and to get to know a place is to stay on the surface—get real hands-on experience. Another reason to avoid light aircraft transportation is for safety. I'm a pilot and so know how dangerous conditions can become in that part of the world. The point was proved eight months later.

The area we were covering, known then as the White Highlands, is about forty thousand square miles—essentially to the east side of Mount Kenya. Joining up with us for the northernmost part of the safari was another extraordinary character. The retired, gun-toting (in the most correct manner) Colonel Hilary Hook. He was a knowledgeable guide—a real white hunter and one of the last of the British Raj (relocated from India) who courted princesses as a sideline. We stayed in hotels, though daytime refreshments were taken en route with Hilary in charge of tables, chairs, umbrellas, and magnificent food, wine, and beer. A common East African practice is to serve tea from a silver pot wherever you are.

One of the hotels we spent the night at was the Mount Kenya Safari Club. Bill Holden was supposed to have been the originator and proprietor, but I understood his role to be purely titular. By the time we were there, it was part of the Intercontinental group. Apart from animal pelts adorning the floors and walls and smiling African waiters, we could have been anywhere in the world. Tourists travel to and from similar accommodations in an air-conditioned bus and for all intents and purposes might just as well be on a sight-seeing tour of Arkansas. Mind you, the view of the snowcapped mountain is hard to find elsewhere. It is one of the places on the equator where it snows. There is a plaque to mark the zero latitude in the hotel's grounds against which thousands upon thousands of visitors have been photographed. I wasn't about to try and prove it, but seemingly the equator was moved to bring it within the premises!

The northernmost point we reached in our rather weary Range Rover was Isiolo, peopled by the regal Samburu tribe. Then east over the Aberdare Mountains—an immense national (wildlife) park rising up to some nine thousand feet. Certainly, at that altitude, we needed very little to drink in the evenings to relax and wash away the dust!

All along the way, we were regaled with intriguing stories from both Monty and Hilary—the mystery surrounding the murder of the Earl of Erroll (as somewhat unexcitingly explored in the film *White Mischief*), the ne'er-do-well sons of Englishmen packed off to the colonies and paid to stay away, and the apparent freedom with which the Europeans interchanged beds. The impression given was that just about everyone had slept with everyone. We learned about the history of the many different tribes, including the ongoing dispute between the predominantly town-dwelling Kikuyu and the nomadic Masai, and about their gods and their philosophy. We also began to discover the ethos of the early European settlers and how they tried to make a go of their lives out there and often failed—coffee plantations were high on the agenda and, in those days, usually did not produce the crop because of blight or unsophisticated farming. We read of Karen Blixen's affair with Dennis Finch-Hatton and his fatal air crash in her autobiography *Out of Africa* and of the much later violent struggles of the Mau-Mau against British domination.

We were getting to the core of the characters that would appear in *Flame Trees*.

The country is very beautiful, but something we were also starting to feel was that, in terms of two-dimensional film, we would have to "sell" Africa in a big way, or it might end up looking like Surrey in England. This notion was firmly dashed as we descended out of the Aberdares and reached the edge of the Rift Valley. The bottom dropped out of the world. This tectonic fault stretches over four thousand miles from the north part of Africa on toward the south. Awesome. And an irresistible backdrop.

We had our scenery; we had our characters, and once back in Nairobi we needed to address the essential involvement of wild animals. The Kenyan laws are rightly very strict about the preservation of their wildlife, but with Monty's help we established a relationship with the animal orphanage. They would help so long as we employed bona fide wranglers. One other point. We were not allowed to kill any (animals not wranglers). Absolutely we agreed to such a moral requirement—although we would have to overcome the scenes requiring such somehow or other.

After three weeks of intensive research (and having a wonderful time along the way), John Hawkesworth and Pussy flew back to London, where he would be finalizing the scripts, which he had decided would be six in total. Meanwhile Malcolm Burgess, Caroline, and I spent three days in Mombasa, where we could rough out a budget for the production and determine what questions still needed to be asked. Christ it was humid! The White Highlands are very hot by day, but it's a dry heat. Personally I was able to step outside our hotel on the Indian Ocean from seven in the morning until about eleven. Thereafter air-conditioning was essential.

And the sea didn't help; it was like getting into a hot bath. Anyway Malcolm and I got a lot of work done before driving the three hundred miles back to Nairobi for final discussions with Monty.

Just one more thing to see . . .

December the twelfth is Kenya's Independence Day. And what a vast jamboree it was. Costumes of every color in the spectrum, dancing, drums, gleaming white teeth, laughter, sun, and plenty of Tusker lager.

No. Windsor Safari Park would never have sufficed!

I have had the misfortune to come across filmmakers who hold the belief that photographs contain enough information to be able to write a script or produce a movie. They could not be more wrong. Essentially writers, producers, and directors must understand everything about a country and its people before attempting to reproduce it on screen. Simply its texture and depth. There is no alternative but to gain the experience. None whatsoever.

We were at Jomo Kenyatta Airport, shortly to board the midnight flight back to London, when tears suddenly started rolling down Caroline's cheeks.

"What's the matter?"

"I've felt it. I've felt the magic. And I don't want to leave."

"It is Eden, isn't it?"

"Yes, it really is."

Our obligation was to present the magic to an audience many thousands of miles away.

Once back in England, Malcolm and I got down to working on a full budget. No thumbnail, this—detail, detail, and more detail. We worked out how every single scene in the completed scripts would be filmed and how rain sequences during the short-rains season could be handled (the rain had to be there at our bidding, not left to the chance downpour covering our location). After several weeks, we had the job completed. For what we were attempting to do, it was a perfectly fair document— not remotely overpriced—with each episode costing around £290,000 (and the series budget at just about £1.75M). This was all right because Thames' contract with our company, Blue Posts Productions, called for a cost of a minimum of £250,000. When John Pringle, Simon Olswang (our legal partner), and John Whitney had originally told me this, I was nothing short of astonished.

"Surely Thames means to say not *more* than £250,000," I had countered.

"See for yourself," Simon said as he handed me the still as-yet unsigned contract.

"That means, in theory, we'd have an unlimited budget."

"Yes, so don't argue the point," put in Messrs. Whitney and Pringle.

"I won't," I replied, slightly bemused.

As well as creative matters still under discussion—including sessions with Elspeth Huxley, whose childhood memories were the basis of the series—there were myriad practical elements now to be considered.

Our plan was to work with two directors—Ferdy Fairfax and Roy Ward Baker (both from *Danger UXB*)—each filming three alternating episodes. It would be tricky for them but manageable and seemed to present the best overall method of production. Once a fifty-minute segment was completed, it could be edited in London while the director prepared for his next film in Africa. Actually all quite neat and tidy.

Two other main points were given our serious attention at this time. First, the casting of a little girl to play Elspeth. She should have been around seven to nine, but to work with one so young would have presented numerous pitfalls with restrictive working hours (she would be in most scenes), education laws, and, not least, taking a female minor to the Dark Continent with a feared reputation of white slave trafficking. So, long before, we had opted to make her eleven years old—at least crossing that threshold allowed us a little more freedom from government restrictions. John Hawkesworth and I spent many, many days trawling the junior performing arts schools across England—normally managing to return home at night. Time went by—February 1980, March, and into April. Our scheduled shooting date of mid-September was still far enough away to give us some space, but the weeks don't half reel by! Manchester, Birmingham, Brighton, the West Country.

Second came the animals. The dead ones, I mean. Unfortunately, dead animals are a natural part of Africa—kill or be killed. There was much to-ing and fro-ing over this as well, but, actually more quickly than we could have hoped, we stumbled across an excellent taxidermist who specialized in African creatures—including pythons. The python turned out to be the least effective, while all the other slain creatures were absolutely convincing.

But it didn't end with dead ones—we needed to find live ones out in open spaces and away from the confinement of the orphanage in Nairobi. To hope that any of them would "read the script" was to hope in vain, and the only way to "see" our actors in scenes involving them was to film the animals in the wild and entirely separately from the principal action. Thankfully the constant, high equatorial light would minimize the question of balance, and the bush could undoubtedly blend in anywhere when it came to matching scenery. We commenced the search for a wildlife cinematographer who could work hand in hand with the directors, who, themselves, could oversee various shots when not occupied with the shooting of one of their episodes.

It was starting to take shape when catastrophe struck. The Thames representative, responsible for contracts, was in Simon Olswang's office with pen raised to sign our (not less than £250,000 per episode) contract when he received a telephone call.

Thames, so often under threat from unreasonable union demands, had been issued with some sort of strike notice by its studio staff. Consequently all future production was to be canceled until the matter was resolved.

"Sorry about that," the representative must surely have said to Simon as he pocketed his fountain pen and departed.

So much effort for nothing—except we had been given a wonderful trip in Kenya as a souvenir.

There was nothing for it but for me to ride our horse Zeebee, a wonderful palomino that had entered our lives after Caroline and I had been through a period of trial separation after *Danger UXB*. I think he was meant to give us a focus outside our immediate relationship. It worked—for a while anyway.

Four weeks or so of silence, and then a call came through from Thames. *Flame Trees* was on again and the now-signed contract was being biked over to Simon Olswang. However, this time the deal was amended to a *maximum* of £250,000 per television hour (someone must have done a bit of rethinking!).

It just wasn't possible though—not the way we had so carefully pieced the show together.

More circuits of Richmond Park for Zeebee and me. And that's when I made up my mind. We would have to find a way of doing the production somehow—it had too much potential to be let go.

When I got home, Caroline told me Ferdy had called.

"Look, I'm sorry," he said. "But I've been offered a smashing two hour drama to direct and with *Flame Trees* looking shaky, I really believe I ought to take it."

"Well, of course you should." I meant it and hoped I had managed to keep the disappointment out of my voice.

That phone call triggered what happened next. Without Ferdy, we had just one director lined up—Roy Ward Baker. Roy was very much for the idea, as he had always wanted to be the sole director—who could blame him? Okay, if we shot all six episodes out of continuity—treating the series as one long (six hour) film, we could cut the schedule from a total of twelve weeks to eleven, and as a result, Malcolm and I reckoned, the overall budget could (because of amortization) be reduced by around £10,000 per episode.

But it wasn't enough—another £30,000 per episode had to go.

Verity had already told us she did not see the necessity of the opening sequence of the whole series. This showed how much like the Wild West Nairobi was in 1912.

"Pioneer Mary," a sassy whiskey-drinking Irish woman, comes into the Blue Posts Hotel—so called because it had blue posts on its veranda. She is on horseback, and, with yelping and whooping aplenty, she starts firing off her guns and stirring up mayhem among the hundred or so settlers around the bar. With fists flying, bottles smashing, and mirrors crashing, it would have been a terrific scene setter—especially with a direct cut to the comparative tranquillity of the open countryside.

However, the cost of the re-created interior set, which ends up half destroyed as a result of the orgy, would be some £15,000 alone. So if we did what Verity suggested and cut the scene, some £2,500-plus could come off each segment. With the greatest of reluctance, John Hawkesworth agreed to its omission.

£27,500 to go.

"Monty," said Malcolm over the phone to Nairobi. "Do you think there's a chance we could find similar locations to the ones we've already seen and liked, but within an hour of the city?"

Monty, normally one of the most positive and helpful of people, hedged his bets this time around. "I wouldn't say 'yes' and I wouldn't say 'no.'"

Immediately Malcolm was despatched to Kenya, where, with any luck, the two of them could establish what we so much needed.

By confining the locations and consequently reducing traveling costs, a potential saving of £10,000 per episode could be made.

Still not enough! £17,500 yet to find.

"We'll be all right," Malcolm reported over a crackly line three days later.

"Thank God for it. But we still need to come down."

Then it suddenly struck me.

"Malcolm, our contract with Euston Films calls for a budget of a 'no more than' amount. But, you know something, it doesn't specify the number of segments."

"True. So what are you getting at?"

"We do seven episodes instead of six."

"Would John ever agree?"

"If it's a make or break situation, he's just going to have to." I went on, "A pound to a pinch of salt, an extra ten days on the overall schedule and an extra £250,000 for the seventh episode must put us on target."

He said he would do some sums on the flight back from Africa.

Ten minutes later—

John Hawkesworth, over the telephone: "Oh, fuck!" he puffed through one of his pernicious cigars.

A week after that, he and I were given lunch in the executive dining room of Thames Television—actually a large motor cruiser (which had played a part in the famous retreat from Dunkirk) moored on the river beside Teddington Studios. All we had to do was reassure them we could make the series under their terms before they raised their glasses and wished us luck.

"See you at the screening," were the last words spoken that day.

Well, the nightmares of the past few weeks had disappeared, and we could afford a brief moment or two to draw breath before getting down to the fine details. And it fell on our production assistant to take the lead. Liz Bunton moved us lock, stock, and barrel into the Euston Films office (on the Euston Road) in spite of some raised eyebrows from the permanent staff.

A nice moment came when Johnny Goodman said he hadn't been instructed to give us the green light from Thames, but Liz simply pointed out that word had been given by the producers that they could meet the obligations of the signed deal. To his credit, Johnny laughed in a confirmatory way and opened his ever-welcoming arms.

But who was to play Elspeth? More scouting around the countryside for Hawkesworth and me. And what about her redoubtable mother Tilly?

"Hayley Mills would be great," said John.

She had been in the first film he had produced—*Tiger Bay*—and he clearly respected her ability. So did I. She had proved herself time and again throughout the 1960s, although by now she had slipped away from the mainstream with motherhood playing an important part in her life.

The idea appealed at once, I really wanted to work with this gifted actress who I had first met thirty-four years earlier, although she denied any knowledge of this, which is hardly surprising, as she was only a few months old at the time. Her parents John Mills and Mary Hayley Bell lived out in the Buckinghamshire countryside just half a mile away from my parents' home. My father and Johnnie had already made several pictures together during the Noël Coward and Cineguild days and had become firm friends, so it was understandable that I should have been invited to his elder daughter Juliet's fifth birthday party. Little children, unaware of the depravations of a very recently war-torn England, laughed and clapped, ate jelly and cake, and all got little presents. For some reason I wandered off and found myself in a bedroom. There, sound asleep in a crib, was a beautiful little baby dressed in white. (For a long time Hayley maintained she was older than me—but neither of us needs to compete over it nowadays.)

At the premiere of *Tiger Bay*, in London's West End, I recall a gorgeous and beautifully presented girl who had the ability to smile winningly and even curtsy delightfully. Hayley has star quality written all over her face. Yes, certainly I must have been a little in love with her—such are the dreams of teenagers. In 1963 my father directed her and Johnnie in *The Chalk Garden*, and on a couple of visits to the set at MGM's Elstree lot, I had the chance to chat briefly with her again.

Now the opportunity presented itself to work with her. Suffice it to say it was to be a pleasure and privilege, although it seems I once caused her a little annoyance. The sometimes-unhappy lot of the producer!

A gold strike.

May 1980.

We found our Elspeth.

Holly Aird was at a school in the south of England. Elmhurst (a nice British name) was a well-regarded stage school—an alumna is Hayley Mills (a nice coincidence).

There was a great similarity between the two. Holly knew how to behave in a genteel way, which was essential for our Elspeth. She had an instinctive sense of fun and was very quick-witted indeed—I even asked her if she could curtsy, as Hayley had done. She could. The past tense is used here because Holly Aird will appear in later pages of this book as an adult actress.

Having selected her—and she and her parents having accepted our proposal—now the only "clincher" was the government license for her to perform—form filling-in, reports, medical examination, working-hours schedule, accommodation, chaperone (her mother) to be approved! Curriculum and place of education (the bush) for when she would be away from her normal schooling. Approved tutor. Endless. And then it would all take a couple of months to process, with, of course, no guarantee a license would be granted. A nail-biting period because, if our application for Holly were turned down, we would be left without a central character and the show would have to have been canceled. What a waste of Thames's money—they would never forgive us.

Crash on regardless and let the devil do his whatever.

Three other main elements to focus on—the cast, animals, and a definitive schedule.

The schedule is always vitally important. This alone dictates the budget; with a given number of weeks of filming, it produces a clear equation. Should the schedule overrun, the budget will overrun—and that's that. The fine-tuning of when crops would naturally yield or adult flame trees would flower and many, many other details were left in the exceptionally capable hands of Clifton Brandon.

Clifton has an innate sense of responsibility—something essential within the makeup of a production manager. In other words, if you can't put to right what's wrong, there is no alternative to hara-kiri. His father had come to England from America and had had a busy life as an assistant director, and so his son learned from an early age the strict need for discipline in the making of films as well as in his personal life (he is an equally disciplined vegetarian whose inadvertent lapse was to cause some amusement in Spain five years hence). His mind is honed to check and double-check all the nuts and bolts—to ensure nothing can go wrong. But such is life—things do go wrong in the ephemeral world of celluloid—and that's when one relies on the experience of a good production manager. Here I must mention that the worst kind of production manager is he or she who is devoid of any creative thoughts. Quietly, subtly, Clifton would raise queries about the substance of the material if he felt it was justified.

If he has a fault, it is the way he "lives" the production with which he is involved during every waking hour, and I swear to God he must do the same while sleeping, thereby limiting his focus on the world around him. Thickly bespectacled and an exacting taskmaster, he has integrity and a sense of humor as arid as can be. He is fastidious, alert, a terrified driver, and, sometimes, a trifle too grumpy, but this man is absolutely splendid. Rolled into one, he can be pictured by the nickname he was dubbed by a member of our team—"Chuckles."

One of his key jobs during preproduction on *Flame Trees* was to cope with the mathematics of putting actors on split-period contracts—when hotel and accommodation costs and per diems outweighed the price of a round-trip air ticket (a come-and-go conundrum that only the best and most meticulous can ever hope to resolve).

The search for a wildlife cameraman finally bore fruit in the guise of a young man named Mike Fox. In spite of his years, he had already become experienced in this kind of work and immediately exuded confidence. Essentially, his would be a three-man team (himself, his assistant, and a tracker) working out in the bush to film animals in their natural habitat. Roy Baker and Mike compiled an extensive shot list whereby both knew what the other was doing so that the cutaways from the principal actors would appear seamless. Occasionally doubles would be used so that our characters could be seen in the same shot as, say, a pride of lions.

The proposed tracker flew over from Kenya to be involved in the planning. This was well before *Crocodile Dundee*, but on reflection he really was a Paul Hogan type. Fearless in the often hostile world of the open African countryside, he was completely at a loss in London—swing doors would slam back on him, motor vehicles bore down on him remorselessly, and the escalators at the Underground stations threatened to chew him up. His task was to sniff out the animals and silently lead Mike to them from downwind.

While these elements were dropping into place, we were also moving ahead with the casting. Once Hayley and Holly were set (the child license still pending), the next to find was someone to play Robin Grant, Elspeth's father. He is a brave and gentle soul but prone to getting himself into debt from making wrong decisions—hence the family's move to Africa to begin a new life. Robin's plan is to start a coffee plantation, and he succeeds in the realization to some extent; however, the crop always fails, and when World War I starts, they return to England. At least they had learned how to handle the often-inhospitable environment, and after the war they would come back and start reaping the benefits of their struggles.

Anthony Andrews was keen to do it and thought he could be available, although currently he was costarring with Jeremy Irons in *Brideshead Revisited*. That production had gone wildly over schedule and had to be halted because Jeremy was required to fulfill a prior commitment to Karel Reisz in *The French Lieutenant's Woman*. If Karel remained on schedule, which he (more or less) undoubtedly would, Tony would have had to go back to *Brideshead* before we could have finished with him in Africa. It would've been lovely to work with him again, but in all honesty he was probably not the best choice of actor. He will hate me for saying it, but, being an extremely good-looking man, he fits more easily into the sophisticated and elegant role rather than the open-air lifestyle of Robin. We finally offered the part to David Robb, who accepted.

With little time to spare, the license for Holly to work finally came through.

East Africa—shooting day minus two.

Oh God! Disaster?

Little Elspeth was supposed to be a natural born rider, but our young leading lady wasn't. Riding lessons before leaving England, yes—an African pony, with the scripted name of Moyale, was a reliable horse that would move only on the filmmakers' command of "Action!"—familiarization of the pair—and THUMP—Holly hit the baked ground hard and after a stunned moment or two burst into tears. The injured child was rushed to the nearest hospital, some forty miles distant in the capital.

I did a rough calculation of all the planning and the amount of money already spent or committed to date and reckoned that a producer's life came cheaper. X-rays—waiting—calming all concerned. And thank God she was all right, nothing broken. So it would be back on the pony for Holly and for me to welcome the vast crew who arrived from London the following day. We had a beginning-of-term party, and I recall saying I must be thought a madman to be producing a series in Africa on a British TV budget at all, let alone with a child and animals as the stars!

Day 1, and the camera took in the breathtaking scenery of East Africa from the side of a hill called Leopard Rock—beneath it the Rift Valley swept away almost as far as the eye could see to the foothills of Mount Kilimanjaro and up to its snowcapped peak. Our characters, the Grant family, arrive on horseback at the site where they would build their new home and establish a farm. Wonderful colors—the azure sky with puffy white clouds mottled with gray, the blue heat haze, the golden green of vegetation, and the indigenous dusty red earth. Actually the latter was one lie. Our principal location was perfect in every respect—visually, for accessibility and proximity to Nairobi, but it didn't have any red earth at all, and without it, it just wouldn't have looked right. So six truckloads of the stuff had been brought in from a few miles away and liberally scattered around the immediate vicinity.

The schedule called for the Grants' house to be fully erected in a total of two and a half days of filming, which would have been physically impossible (what with the mud on wattled walls requiring time to dry out) had set designer Roy Stannard not come up with a ruse. First, there was an area of leveled ground with strings marking out where the walls would go. We shot the necessary scenes on this, essentially favoring the view across the valley. Then the next day we moved back forty yards and to the left where the completed outline of the house had already been readied. Roy had also made a three-foot-high, red termite mound out of polystyrene that was judiciously repositioned from the initial plot to realign with the second phase. On the third day we did the same thing on a completed and dried-out house. The termite mound was the continuity reference, while the vista remained as near as exactly the same from all three positions.

At least the first week of principal photography remained on target. Actually with proper discipline, it is hard to fall behind schedule on the equator and even harder to go into expensive overtime—the sun literally drops out of the sky at 6:00 P.M., and darkness is everywhere by 6:30. "Go home" is the reading on a light meter!

Caroline was due to make a second trip out to Kenya to join me for a couple of weeks' holiday—she had produced a small film for children which was ready for delivery—but she demurred. I knew something was wrong, especially as our marriage had been going through a rocky patch for a couple of years. All a bit complicated—both of us had come together on the rebound, me from a failed first marriage, which had seen the birth of three wonderful children, and Caroline from a strong relationship with a married man. Now he was divorced, and my own eyes had strayed, and consequently our "union" began to fall asunder. (Divorce was to follow two years later and thankfully without the tiniest bit of acrimony—she and I stay in contact to this day, meet up, and have long conversations on the telephone. The truth is we love each other very much, and I greatly appreciate her continued support and hopefully vice versa, but we should never have been man and wife.)

Tricky relationships were par for the course in the lives of the early Kenyan settlers, and one of the strands of *Flame Trees* deals with this nicely. Nicholas Jones gave a beautifully measured performance as the aloof Hereward Palmer, who has come to Africa with his young wife Lettice (Sharon Mughan—later Maughan). Here they hope to reestablish their relationship after her philandering back in Europe. They build a grand home and begin to develop their farm, but Hereward is completely inept at handling the Africans, and failure is inevitable. So too the recovery of their marriage when Lettice falls into the arms of a white hunter, perfectly played by Ben Cross. Ben had recently starred as Harold Abrahams in *Chariots of Fire*.

Roy Stannard designed the Palmers' house on a cleared site in the arid bush nearby to our Leopard Rock location, and it was equal to anything that might have been found in the emerging Beverly Hills of the early twentieth century.

"The set has burned down," exclaimed John Hawkesworth in some justifiable alarm as he hurried into my office back at the base in Nairobi. "What are you going to do about it?"

Even though this was a serious disaster, I remembered the rule of never pressing "the panic button"—it was a lesson instilled into me when, back in my twenties, I had learned to fly.

"Is the fire brigade on its way?"

"They've been called." Which meant someone had driven back to the city from the location to request the services of the one fire truck owned and operated by Nairobi.

"Better get out there," advised John.

"I will."

But before I did, I called in to Clifton in the production office.

"Don't know anything about it," he said.

"Why not?" I demanded.

"No one's told me."

"I'm telling you now!"

As he seemed more concerned with penciling minor amendments to the schedule with a stubby pencil (Clifton seems to prefer stubby, yellow pencils), I opted to hurry on my way.

At least there was no pall of smoke to be seen from twenty miles away—ten—five—one.

I pulled up outside the Palmer's house and everything looked all right—Roy going about the final details of set dressing.

"Where's the fire?"

"What fire?" he asked laconically.

Hawkesworth had "set me up," and I'd fallen prey—eighty miles round trip for nothing!

Back in Nairobi, I waited until it was time for him to pop by my office for an evening drink—and I was well prepared.

"God, I thought you were joking about the fire at the Palmers'."

He chortled.

"But thankfully it's not too serious."

"What do you mean?" There was a degree of doubt in his expression.

"Couple of days and we'll have it repaired."

He didn't know whether to believe me—probably not.

"Help yourself to a scotch."

He did so.

"Soda's in the 'fridge'."

He unscrewed the top slowly—at an altitude of five thousand feet, soda is inclined to be hyperactive. Particularly so on this occasion, as I had given the bottle a good shake. John Hawkesworth was drenched—certainly put his fire out.

To my mind and indeed my generation's mind, the playing of practical jokes (if not too unkind) was an essential part of everyday life. There are many, many pressures that go along with any form of filmmaking, and pressure needs relieving. A laugh at the right moment can be a salvation at little cost. In our case gasoline to cover a few miles and a bottle of soda.

John was on the location for a very brief period and essentially remained back in London for most of the production to review the daily processed footage and supervise the assembly of the material. He and Liz Bunton kept in good contact throughout, and I could address any hiccups encountered at their end immediately, and naturally the reverse applied. Verity Lambert, wisely equipped with a solar topee, joined John on his sojourn. This was very good, as it allowed us to get to know each other better. Verity is one of a kind. She has the wonderful ability to see what is going on around her, to understand where people come from, to understand what makes them tick. Instinctively she knows when a character on a scripted page is honest to him- or herself, and she has a built-in sense of dramatic rhythm. Many have tried to emulate her, and many have been good seconds—seconds. I found our conversations together stimulating both in terms of business and as individuals. At this time we were still in the man's world with the few leading, lady executives having to fight their corners against misogyny. In my experience three of them handled this effortlessly while remaining utterly feminine (no swearing just to keep up with the boys, elegant dressing, and quiet persuasion). Joan Harrison (Alfred Hitchcock's TV series producer), Mai Zetterling (actress turned director), and Verity. I am privileged to have worked with all three.

"Exactly, what does a producer do?" asked the wise little Holly Aird of me one morning. This child's eyes were everywhere.

"That's a very hard question to answer whilst at the same time being easy."

"What do you mean?" she quizzed.

"Look," I said, "ask me again in three weeks and I'll tell you."

"Is it . . . ?"

"Shhh . . ." I raised a finger. "Three weeks."

At least it would give me time to come up with an answer to what was actually quite a tricky question.

Holly was/is astonishing. Her power of learning and recollection is incredible, and she certainly gained more knowledge about life from her thirteen or so weeks in Africa than she could ever have done from a classroom in England. An invaluable experience for her.

There are many examples of the sharpness of her mind, but let one suffice for now. Holly knew the dialogue of every character in all seven episodes and could recite any line out of continuity whenever.

We viewed our rushes or dailies on the newly introduced VCR, which saved our precious budget the cost of shipping processed and synchronized material back out to Africa. This, however, was unfair to the director, cinematographer Ian Wilson and designer Roy Stannard—they needed to see some quality reproduction of their work. So occasionally film (not sound) was dispatched for projection in Nairobi. On one session little Holly stood behind the screen—the lower half of her legs apparent beneath it, and she postsynchronized the dialogue for every actor, giving a good performance into the bargain.

"So what do producers do? You promised to tell," she said when the three weeks were up.

"Yes, I did. The answer is nothing."

"That's not a proper answer."

"It is."

"Then you are going to have to explain it to me."

"Once a production is financed, a producer oversees the whole business right from the start, and if everyone does everything exactly as they are supposed to, there is nothing to be done."

"And if they don't do it exactly right?"

"Then the producer is there to help them back on track. But usually they do do it right."

Largely speaking, it was a true enough answer; nevertheless, it helps to be a "jack-of-all-trades."

And thank God for the likes of Clifton to give proper backup.

The production manager's role tends to be office based in order to get a clear overview of what is to come some days or weeks ahead. It is the job of the assistant director to handle matters on set on a day-by-day basis. A common misunderstanding about this job is that such a person is in second command of the actual direction of the actors and crew. No—the task is that of a stage manager/floor manager in live television and is 90 percent concerned with the efficient management of the shooting crew. It is true the ideal candidate for this is most probably of a different makeup to the production manager—more outgoing, an instinctive performer with instantly engaging communication skills—yet tough when needs be.

On *Flame Trees* we had a past master—Gino Marotta. With a name like his, one might be forgiven for imagining he was an attractive Mediterranean type—no, not our Gino. A big man in every sense of the word with fairish curly hair, he was a product of London's East End and had a ripe Cockney accent to prove it. One of his most used lines before the start of a shot was the instruction to the African extras who were playing the laborers clearing the land around the Grants' farm. "Workin' away in the background boys."

I had a quiet word in his ear about it. "Gino, you ought to be a bit careful—they resent being called "boys.'"

"Oh, yeah—or-right, Guv."

Next shot, "Workin' away in the background boys."

I winced, but somehow, because of his good sense of humor, he got away with what most could not. The extras loved him.

We were filming a hunting sequence and had several Africans acting as spotters—often up in a tree. After one shot was completed and the crew had started moving elsewhere, I noticed a man still left there in the boughs and pointed him out to Gino.

"Oola-ngoola jambo shamba," he called up to the chap, who instantly knew that Gino's gobbledygook Swahili meant "come down." He was able to communicate with anyone simply because of his strength of personality, although he didn't want much to do with his assistant when the young man was unlucky enough to contract hepatitis.

"Should have taken more care of hisself."

Not really fair—infected water.

It was this illness that prompted me to get the entire cast and crew inoculated against the disease with a shot called gamma globulin. It was painful to receive but was rumored to do wonders for the libido. I recall seeing about seventy-five people lining up to get the jab and wondering what little adventures between them would come about. Mind you there is no aphrodisiac like being on a foreign location in the first place, and liaisons are not uncommon. The film industry has a bad reputation here, which it is incumbent on me to defend. Certainly many businesses take personnel to far-flung places—engineers lay pipelines in the Sahara, oilmen work on rigs, construction workers build dams. We are not unique for sure, but we do employ men and women in equal numbers, and often these are people in high profile—the rest follows. Enough!

On a Sunday about halfway through our schedule, Elspeth Huxley flew out from England to see how we were getting on with the retelling of her childhood life. A splendid reception was planned for the evening, and we were all looking forward to it—though for me the day didn't start too well.

The previous week, the *Kenya Times* had interviewed me in connection with the series and asked how agreeable we were finding filming in the country. Sunday headline—"Film Producer Slams the Government." It was all to do with dear old Monty Ruben. He had set up the meeting in the first place and had been present at lunch with the journalist. Aware of how careful one has to be about the feelings of so many African nations, I had been on my best behavior and praised all and sundry, but "Mont" used it to highlight a tax on foreign filmmakers he considered nefarious. This was a levy on raw film stock entering the country and paid in advance for the privilege of capturing the beautiful scenery. Believing it to discourage the local industry's growth, he had made the point gently enough, but give a journalist an inch etcetera!

Throughout that Sunday I expected the police to arrive and escort me to the airport. Fortunately it didn't come to pass, and I subsequently received congratulations from many in Nairobi's tourist and business community for speaking out as "I" had. All honors to Monty.

Although having spent most of her life in her native England, Elspeth had remained in physical contact with her adoptive country throughout the years, and consequently she was feted wherever she went. It was a pleasure to see this still ebullient octogenarian welcomed in such a way, and it was a terrific tonic for the cast and crew to have her on set—the midpoint of filming is when a company's energy is at its nadir. In reality it didn't get too low on *Flame Trees*. Cinematographer Ian Wilson saw to that.

He is an excellent cameraman if for nothing other than the simplicity with which he approached filming on the equator. He requested a manageable amount of lights for interior scenes but "had" to have two "brutes" (arc lights) for the exteriors (called brutes because of their size and weight).

"Brutes!" yelped our production manager. "Can't afford them."

"He's got a good point, Clifton," I had responded. "High sun, and with everyone wearing hats their faces will be thrown into shadow, and all the Europeans will end up on screen looking like Kikuyu warriors."

"Humphhh!"

"Ian will use them like 'bashers' to fill the shadows and can cover a wide area into the bargain. Speedier in the long run."

"Why not reflectors? We can afford plenty of those."

"They wobble in the wind, and we'll end up making something looking akin to a spaghetti western."

Ian got his brutes, and we remained on schedule.

Light, longish hair; vivid blue eyes; and a huge laugh usually concluding with a bit of wheezing and a cough (not a smoker as it happens), Ian is the epitome of a well-educated Englishman—courteous, attentive, thorough, and with a sense of fun still at the teen level (I've had several water pistol fights with him). Professionally he is adept at creating a visual atmosphere—dust motes caught in the light from a small, high window in a chapel; shadows from a wattle wall subtly placed across a face; and a soft light on the faces of women even in the harshest of the noonday suns. Deservedly he was to receive a BAFTA nomination for his work on this series.

Only one near catastrophe with him (excluding the air crash, that is). The end sequence of the series, filmed out of continuity, shows young Elspeth and Tilly following Robin Grant back to England at the outbreak of the Great War. By then the railway had reached as far as Thika, and so we had to have a train. This was arranged by Malcolm Burgess (now an associate producer) using adept negotiation when it came to Kenyan officialdom. He stayed on the case for nine months and got away with only one bribe (a Polaroid camera with a few packs of film—actually the only bribe we succumbed to in a reportedly bribe-ridden country). The ideal period steam engine (converted to diesel) was, by the latter part of the twentieth century, relegated to shunting trucks up near Lake Victoria. Malcolm finally persuaded those in places of power that its presence in Nairobi was essential—particularly if the government wanted an extra tourist attraction! Rolling stock was brought out of mothballs from Nairobi's fledgling railway museum by laying a hundred yards of track to give it access to the main line.

And there it all was on the appointed day. Steam huffing and puffing (in reality smoke canisters), an Indian engineer (frowned on by new Kenya), and two crossed Union Jacks of Great Britain emblazoning the front (even more frowned on).

Long shot—camera way back and high—Ian Wilson scurrying through the assembled European and African extras in search of the company's painter.

Once found, he gave an instruction that was fortunately overheard by Malcolm.

"Change the U.R. (Uganda Railways) sign on the tender to K.R."

"No," shrieked Malcolm, "Kenya didn't have any trains then—just the line from Mombasa!"

By November the short rains were due to arrive, and that was when those scenes taking place during the season were scheduled to be shot. The name implies a limited period of downpour, which is absolutely right, and in places freely selected by the elements. Whereas the sky around our location looked spectacular all the time, there was no guarantee the rain would fall when and where we wanted, so Nairobi's sole fire truck was deployed. Everyone thought we were crazy—"Typical film company nonsense! Pahh!!"

Its presence was essential—we needed rain under our immediate control, and we got it from powerful hoses squirted upward, although half a dozen tankers had to bring city water out to the location—no risk of drenching our actors with bilharzia infected water.

Ian Wilson did something very cunning with one shot. The principal characters were trundled along in an open motorcar—soaked of course. Once the shot was in the "can," Ian requested another take with the camera's lens aperture fully open, thus vastly overexposing the image. All that needed to be done was to cut a few frames of this into the main shot at an appropriate time, and lo and behold! there was a brilliant flash of lightning (and it didn't have to be exactly matching "action" as the eye shifts slightly under such circumstances).

Getting caught in a real tropical downpour can be pretty frightening at any time, but nothing like the experience Ian, camera operator Peter Sinclair, and Malcolm Burgess faced one evening.

A location we were to use was around two hundred miles up country near Isiolo. This really was a case of the mountain going to Mohammed, as the entire unit would be relocated for the opening sequences, which would show Tilly and Elspeth traveling to Thika for the first time. It wasn't the scenery dictating the site but the oxen. They were called upon to draw a wagon loaded with the Grants' possessions shipped out from England. In modern times it is nigh on impossible to find a trained team of "beasts of burden" and even harder to track down anyone who could get them into some sort of working order. We had ultimately been lucky in our search and through Monty had met David

Craig, who, with his wife, ran a tented safari camp at Lewa Downs. For nine months he trained a team to pull a rumbling wagon along specifically chosen tracks. To have got so many heavy animals (unpanicked) down to Nairobi and retrained there was a far bigger deal than us getting ourselves to them; besides, the risk of foot-and-mouth disease would have precluded it in any event.

Two weekends before our move, Ian, Peter, and Malcolm (along with our production assistant who went for the ride) did a survey, and as they didn't have time to drive there and back in the day, they were authorized to take a charter flight directly to the landing strip at Lewa Downs.

Apparently a good time was had by all, and with the work completed they took off again at around 4:30 P.M. It was getting dark by the time they were overhead Nairobi—darker than usual because of a thunderstorm and lashing rain. The lady pilot of their twin-engine Piper decided to divert from the destination airstrip—coincidentally called Wilson—to the capital's Jomo Kenyatta International Airport because it had an instrument landing system. They had just turned onto the final approach when the Wilson Tower called them to say the storm had passed. They diverted again, and ten minutes later, in pitch darkness and with nothing to help them in but the runway's landing lights, they started the descent. You can imagine it—150 feet . . . airspeed dropping back to eighty knots . . . full flaps . . . fifty feet . . . over the hedge . . . twenty-five feet . . . speed back . . . ten feet . . . flaring out . . . WALLOP!

The plane had hit some sort of mound, bounced off the top, slowed perhaps to thirty knots as it slewed onto the laterite strip with its landing gear ripped off. It transpired that some bright spark had decided to dig up the runway and no one had bothered to tell the pilot!

Thank God none was seriously injured—just a sprained back for poor Malcolm and a bit of depression a few days later for all of them.

So much for aerial surveys!

Hayley Mills wasn't very pleased with me as she and David Robb and the entire cast had, on my instruction, been told they had to spend the whole of every working day out on the principal location (all of an hour away from base). However unpopular this was, it was a decision based on logic. Two weeks of the schedule remained to be completed, and what with the capriciousness of the rains, we had to be ready to shoot whatever we could at any time. It may have been interiors of the Grants' house—day or night scenes. Sunny exteriors or rainy exteriors. Anything the elements selected for us.

I explained this carefully to Hayley, and she admitted it made sense, although she and most of the others were not too happy—still they wanted to be home for Christmas.

Dai Bradley, with whom I had worked before (and have done since), was totally sanguine. On a previous occasion this gentle soul had been "called" for first thing one morning even though he was unlikely to be used that day. The reason he was there was in case a scene involving animals proved impossible to shoot and we had to switch to a scene featuring him. Unfortunately he hadn't been told of the plan, and by the evening he was weary with boredom.

"You see," he said to me, "if I'd known I probably wouldn't be used, I'd have gone prepared with a couple of books." He had a fair point. Too often actors are left hanging around as they try to keep their performance energy level up, and it is only reasonable to let them know what is happening. Certainly Dai got through several books during the last two weeks.

The animal sequences were all coming together well, and Mike Fox's footage was cutting into Roy Baker's principal photography as neatly as we had hoped. But all the time we had to strive to get our characters (or doubles) in the same shot as the animals as often as possible. One effective method used went like this:

EXT. BUSH. DAY. (Roy Baker shot with principal actors.)
   Four or five people come to a stop and look off camera left.
EXT. WIDE CLEARING. DAY. (Mike Fox shot filmed in the Masai Mara.)
   A herd of grazing buffaloes.
EXT. BUSH. DAY. (R. B. shot with principal actors.)
   One of the group moves forward again.
EXT. WIDE CLEARING. DAY. (M. F. shot using a double.)
   Apparently a reverse angle with the person moving up to take cover near some trees. Buffaloes beyond him.
EXT. BUSH AND TREES. DAY. (R. B. shot with principal actors.)

*The remainder of the group move up behind him. Continue to watch
the (off-screen) animals.*
EXT. WIDE CLEARING. DAY. (M. F. shot—buffaloes only.)
*Suddenly the buffaloes get wind of the intruders. Panic. Various shots
of the now stampeding beasts.*
EXT. BUSH AND TREES. DAY. (R. B. shot with principal actors.)
The group realizes the buffaloes are going to come right by them.
INTERCUTS . . .
EXT. BUSH AND TREES. DAY. (R. B. shot with principal actors.)
LOW ANGLE. *Everyone pulls back tightly. Fear on their faces as the
creatures thunder by. Swirling dust.*

(The above is not from John Hawkesworth's screenplay and, as once
before, is presented here merely to illustrate how the sequence went
together.)

The last shot was achieved by filming from a low angle and driving
black domestic cows past the camera—only their blurred legs could be
seen.

A similar method was employed for an elephant charge (no legs
though). In reality this is one of the most frightening things in Africa
with the elephants pushing anyone or anything out of the way with
their enormous tusks. Added to this, they make a terrifying noise—a
deep rumble created somewhere deep inside them.

When we came to the postproduction stage, something rather good
happened with the scene. The editors had found sound tracks of this
sort of roar mixed with trumpeting; meanwhile the composers Ken
Howard and Alan Blaikley had come up with a musical version. Which
to use? Naturally the editors wanted the real thing, but I asked them to
try using both.

"You can't do that. It has to be one or the other."

"No harm in trying."

Wow! The clashing sounds and the images came to life in a way
none of us had expected. There is no way the charge could have been
more dramatic.

By the end of the first week of December 1980, the filming was all
over. And there was not a person who didn't shed a little tear. It had

been one of the most wonderful experiences life could offer—we had been paid as well!

Postscript

The Knowledge did very well in the United Kingdom and was nominated by BAFTA as Best Single Drama. Fortunately I was on a flight to Kenya on the evening of the awards ceremony, and on arrival at Nairobi's Norfolk Hotel, I received a kind and thoughtful note from Liz Bunton ending with, "Better luck next time." I didn't mind we hadn't won—the real thrill is to be nominated by one's peers, and who cares about the final, fine-line outcome? It sounds like "sour grapes," but I assure you it is not the case; simply, I far preferred being in Africa on the start of an exciting new project than attending a function with plumped-up, dinner-jacketed executives and pouting, eyebrow-plucked ladies from both sides of the camera. Some years later, when nominated for another film, I didn't want to attend a similar occasion but was dragged there by my wife, who (and I suspect rightly) said it was my responsibility to be present. These events are self-congratulatory—rather smug—and, frankly, long-winded.

Shortly we learned that PBS wanted to play *The Knowledge* on American TV. Astonishing. With the thick London accents, it seemed appropriate to dub it into American! Still it was very well received, and New Yorkers remember it today. Countless times, when chatting to a cabbie about his or her London Carriage Office experiences, we get to talk about the film. They've all seen it, check it out for yourself one day, and all have had fares from American tourists who have asked them about *The Knowledge*. One person who didn't see it was the Mr. Finlay, the real Carriage Office examiner—sadly he died before the transmission.

My son, Gareth, viewed the film on video every time he was with me between the ages of twelve and seventeen, which, I suspect, means he has seen it more times than the combined number of all of us who put it together ever did. Undoubtedly this piece of television filmmaking influenced him into the world of television drama.

Only one thing lets it down—16 mm. I will not moan about this any more but am happy to say that very soon we were able to shoot a series on the proper 35 mm.

The Flame Trees of Thika was also very well received in both the United Kingdom and the United States with good reviews and good viewing figures. Undoubtedly the wonderful music by Howard and Blaikley put the icing on the cake. The main theme is led by African pipes. (Actually, they were South American, but who's counting?) So popular was it that it's become a standard. You hear it played in restaurants and elevators—once it was even piped out before and after take-off on an Iberia flight I was on.

Elspeth Huxley had written a sequel called *The Mottled Lizard*, which is set just after the Great War, and we very much wanted to film this, but Verity was not keen. It was disappointing at the time, but I expect she had good reasons—she usually does—probably she wanted to pioneer more work rather than going down the same path. The subject raised its head again during the mid-1980s heyday of John Pringle's Consolidated Productions. It would have been good then because Holly Aird was just at the right age and a lot of the old team wanted to get back on board. But it wasn't to be.

Shortly after *Flame Trees* was aired, an old chum, Terry Clegg, took Liz Bunton and me to lunch in order to pick our brains about filming in Kenya. He was about to join Sidney Pollack for Karen Blixen's autobiography *Out of Africa*. We were able to point him in the direction of Monty Ruben for a start. My agent in America didn't know why anyone would want to make this film, and it was reported back to me that he had told a number of people that Hawkesworth and Neame had already made the definitive African film. But time moves on.

Ephemera . . .

Karen Blixen had a "kitchen toto" called Kamante Gatura, who appears in both her book and as a character in the film. He was in his eighties by the time he played a small part in our series. This man had been born in a land that did not even have the wheel (true) and had seen it develop through to the days of jumbo jets.

Trivial Pursuit. Who was the star of The Flame Trees of Thika? *I answered, "Holly Aird." "No, Hayley Mills." So be it.*

Two tips for animal handlers (probably illegal nowadays):

To keep chickens in the same spot for continuity purposes, hold them tightish and swing them around a couple of times and position them where required on set. They are too dizzy to move for ten minutes.

When filming with a python, put it in a wet sack and hang it on a clothesline overnight so it goes into a deep sleep. If filming over several days, get more than one python.

CHAPTER THREE

~

Quite Easily Done

Or *Quod erat demonstrandum*—a mathematical summation, "that which was to have been proved is now proven." Or Quentin Everhard Deverill. In our case it meant all three.

Since involving himself with television production in 1979, John Pringle had been determined to enter Consolidated (née Blue Posts Productions) into the American TV network world, and he set his sights on Bill Paley (apparently a longtime family friend), who was still the Grand Master of CBS at the age of eighty. Paley introduced John to one of the broadcaster's vice presidents—New York–based Alan Wagner.

With *Flame Trees* winding down, Hawkesworth's creativity was already working on a new idea that would have an American actor (de rigueur) in the leading role of what was hoped would be a long-running series. Professor Deverill is a visionary physicist at Harvard with a highly investigative mind—if you will, a sort of amateur sleuth who uses his scientific background to solve worldwide threats to the stability of life. His constant opponent is Dr. Stefan Kilkiss (a name plucked from an atlas—Kilkis in Macedonia). A middle European, with an equally brilliant mind, he is an antagonist in the vein of Sherlock Holmes' Moriarty. The series, which is set in England and on the

European continent, takes place during the period, now well explored by us, just before World War I.

The pilot episode shows Deverill revealing to his Harvard colleagues the concept of television and how images could be transmitted through the air. He is laughed off the podium. Testy by nature, he storms out of the American way of life and opts to settle in an ancient pile in England left to him by an aged aunt. On his arrival in London, he hails a taxi, but the driver does not want to take him way out into the sticks. So Deverill buys the cab from him there and then and, with the bemused man sitting in the back of his (own) cab, tears away to pastures new. Phipps ends up as his servant and cohort. Soon a young woman becomes his secretary—and along comes one of his ex-students, who is working as a journalist in the United Kingdom. A series of incidents (including being wrecked at sea) lead them to the Friesland coast, where they confront Kilkiss. This evil man has devised a rocket for Kaiser Wilhelm to fire at London—a foretaste of what was in reality to befall the city thirty years later during the German Blitzkrieg.

After initially being held captive, Deverill and his team of "goodies" manage to foil the plan by blowing up the rocket and its bunker before escaping immediate danger in the kaiser's car with a troop of Uhlan in hot pursuit. They finally get away in a hot-air balloon. From the above, it should by now be clear we were making a spoof! To underscore this, later episodes had titles such as *The 4:10 to Zurich* and *The Limehouse Connection*.

Alan Wagner had commissioned the pilot script in early 1981 but had insisted on having an American co-screenwriter. Hawkesworth unquestionably took the leading role, but, entirely understandably, he did not know the whys and wherefores of U.S. network TV. By May, Alan had approved the script and green-lighted its production on a budget of some $1.5 million. This was a lot of money by our standards, but we would need it if we stood a chance of competing with other series.

Casting got under way immediately with CBS concentrating on the two American characters, Deverill and his ex-student Charlie Andrews. Several names came forward, but none could surpass the unique Sam Waterston as the former—gladly he was up for it. And A. C. Weary was suggested and approved by the network for the other role, someone we new little about.

Work permits would be required for them both. Obtaining one for Sam was a forgone conclusion because, having worked in England before, he was already recognized by Equity, on whose word the Department of Employment acts. But it was a different matter when it came to Mr. Weary. Rather as with the Holly Aird license, the processing of applications can take several weeks with absolutely no guarantee of a successful outcome—Equity has always had a strong North American arm, and those members of the union already resident in England would prefer to see one of their number engaged as opposed to a visitor. What to do? If he was turned down (and there was precedent for this—even to the point of productions being canceled at vast expense), how could we ever find a replacement at the eleventh hour who would meet with CBS's approval?

Only one thing for it, I invited the civil servant responsible for such matters at the Department of Employment to lunch at Twickenham Studios—they enjoy a day out of London as well as the environment of the entertainment world. He turned out to be the understanding sort.

"Can you put your hand on your heart and tell me that without this American actor the series will be canceled?" he asked.

"Almost. What I can say is it would 'more than likely' be canceled."

"Meaning the loss of employment for everyone else involved in the production."

"Exactly."

"How many people, approximately?"

"Directly—eighty or ninety—indirectly double the number," I replied.

"Then I'll tell you what we'll do. Let the Equity process continue as it should, and if Mr. Weary is blocked, we will use our right to override the decision. Acceptable to you?"

What an enjoyable lunch it was.

In the final event, "AC" was to invest in the part the avidness of youth with a natural yearning for adventure—in a way there is an element of the Jimmy Stewart gaucheness about him with his ever-engaging smile.

In England we secured the services of the very funny George Innes to play Phipps—he had been one of our Royal Engineers sappers in *Danger UXB* and had worked with John before on *Upstairs, Downstairs*. Sarah

Berger joined us as the young woman, who, although probably secretly in love with Deverill, was destined to remain his platonic friend. Kilkiss was a fun part to cast. The first actor we chose dropped out when it came to negotiations, and at the last minute I contacted Julian Glover—someone I had worked with fifteen or more years before. Kilkiss is chameleon-like, his guises changing to fit in with whomsoever he has tricked into sponsoring his outlandish and demonic exploits—for example, a Tyrolean count or a Japanese businessman with round, thin-framed spectacles.

Once the principal cast was lined up, Alan Wagner, who is a terrific guy and a first-rate executive, did, however, leave me "gob-smacked" after one telephone conversation.

"All we have to think about now," he said, "is how we get to see the 'dailies' in New York."

It was certainly not all we had to think about. First, there were the practical matters of filming and where? These things had to be left largely in the eminently capable hands of Malcolm Burgess, Clifton Brandon, and Liz Bunton—my task with the help of Maggie Cartier, the casting director, and Simon Olswang, Consolidated's lawyer, was to devise some sort of long-term option contract with the actors. The Americans would be working within the parameters of their guild agreements, but for the British contingent it was going to be breaking new ground, as "option contracts" did not exist. (Normally a U.K. series would continue on by "gentlemen's agreement.")

Standard network deals with producers are unilateral. If a show gets enough in the way of ratings, it could proceed with (normally) twenty-two segments "ordered" per year for five years or more—a couple of rating points up, and that could increase to a greater annual output. Drop two points, and it was off the air. So clearly we had to keep the cast in place for a long time without having to pay them if the show was not a success—a five-year (again unilateral) contract—whoops.

What at first appeared to be a stumbling block was that British Actors' Equity was currently not talking to the British Film and Television Producers Association (subsequently PACT)—the organization responsible for negotiations. Ultimately this turned to our advantage—I was able to go directly to the union and make a one-off agreement for QED. Each actor would be paid for the pilot, after which they remained on a second (nonexclusive) call to us for three months for a set retainer—we considered three months to be long enough for CBS to make a series order. If they did not, the actors would be released. The same would apply for every season with a pre-arranged escalator clause. It was also necessary to "buy out" repeat fees in accordance with the CBS/Consolidated contract. It all worked beautifully, although disappointment for one of the cast lay ahead.

Another snag: the Directors' Guild of America was about to call a strike, and the chances of finding a nonmember whom the network would approve was asking rather a lot. I trawled through various directories and ticked a dozen possibilities.

"No, sorry, Chris—I'm DGA."

"'Fraid I can't—DGA."

"Love to do it, but it's impossible for me."

"I'd be chucked out of the DGA forever."

And so on.

I was getting near to the end of the alphabetical list when . . .

"No idea why I never joined, but I didn't," said Don Sharp.

Bingo!

I had done several pictures with Don when I was a clapper boy. An Australian by birth and a laugher by nature, he was perfect. This actor turned director's list of movies is impressive—*Bear Island* with Donald Sutherland and Vanessa Redgrave, *Thirty-Nine Steps* starring Robert Powell, *Hennesy* with Rod Steiger and Lee Remick, etcetera. Experienced in filming action sequences—for example, *Puppet on a Chain* and *Those Magnificent Men in Their Flying Machines*—he was well equipped to handle our action work. Alan Wagner agreed. (Now all we had to do was figure out how we got the dailies to New York. Joy of joys—CBS insisted they would be on 35-mm film!)

With Don's help, the rest of the pilot's cast dropped into place, and many of the crew members who had been on *Flame Trees* came along for the tiny three-week schedule—two weeks in Twickenham Studios and a week on the north Norfolk coast (doubling as Friesland).

By the height of summer everything was in place, and our two American actors arrived in London. Also coming over from the States were Ron Austin and Jim Buchanan as supervising producers, a bit of an odd title because neither had anything to do with production—that was for John Hawkesworth and me to handle. No, their role was to supervise writers and start working on story lines for later episodes.

I must record here and now—the American foursome on *QED* was a delight to work with. Sam is a thoughtful man, his eyes ever twinkling. As an actor he is both word and performance perfect and never once created any fuss or bother. He does not see himself as the star hanging above all others; rather, he prefers to be one of the team. In the role of Deverill, he created a wonderful character—incisive mind when it came to scientific matters or analyzing the criminal machinations of Kilkiss and other villains but utterly chaotic in any kind of personal management area.

"I can't find my passport," he tells Phipps rather crossly.

"Have you looked in the filing cabinet under 'P'?"

"Yes."

Phipps finds it under "S"—Switzerland was the last country Deverill had visited.

Sam was also entirely convincing as the potty inventor—a jet-powered car for instance. How easy it would have been for him to go over the top with some of the material—he never did. And he managed to keep the audience with him even when Deverill is at his most irascible—usually brought about because of his impatience with himself. He gave the eponymous hero tremendous drive and enthusiasm. I have been lucky enough to have worked with many great actors—Alec Guinness, Bob Mitchum (I shall not continue to name-drop)—and I would have to say Sam is right at the very top of the tree.

Although Hawkesworth remained at the helm with subsequent scripts, both Austin and Buchanan contributed greatly. Their network experience includes the original *Charlie's Angels* and *McCloud*. Ron is probably more of an Anglophile than Jim and was able to relate well with British writers, while Jim, who would be based in Los Angeles, brought the cutting edge of American sensibilities to the material.

Attempting to bridge the Atlantic was fun (although dangerous)—whereas we tend to say the Japanese motorcar industry is a commercial threat from the East, in the United States it is a commercial threat from the West! The United Kingdom has taps; America has faucets (pronounced "foss-its" as opposed to "fore-setts"). And then we had the opportunity for the George Innes character to educate Deverill in the art of cockney rhyming slang where the end of a phrase rhymes with the word it actually means: trouble and strife = "wife," Brahms and Liszt =

"pissed," Bristol City = "titty." There are thousands, and we even thought of marketing a "Mr. Phipps English Dictionary."

It seemed that no sooner had we started filming the pilot than it was all over. The hot, sandy beaches of Norfolk reminiscent of Malibu on an inconceivably quiet day and the cool of the Twickenham sound-stages offering welcome relief. The result of all our efforts was a promising start toward the highly competitive network market.

Hawkesworth and me off to Los Angeles by late summer, screening with executives, including Alan Wagner in from New York. Everyone seemed to love the show—witty and original—nearly everyone, I should say, as one of our team thought it overproduced. I'm not absolutely sure what was meant but presume it referred to the production values—hell yes, then it was certainly and rightly overproduced! There and then CBS offered us a so-called short order (with fixed transmission dates on Monday evenings in March 1982)—that's to say, five more episodes to act as a sort of fuller pilot and hopefully lead to greater things still. Euphoria! Drinks all round—we had done it—or had we?

The first blow was when we were asked to recast the part of Deverill's companion-cum-secretary. There is no question, Sarah Berger had done a good job, but physically or for reasons of personality she was deemed not to be the type of girl they would go for in, say, Williams, Arizona. Terribly unfair—a prejudgment—but we had no choice in the matter. Of course we spoke to Sarah personally to express our sorrow, yet her option contract could not be exercised. (Soon she moved on to other things and has had a prolific career since.) The role was to be taken on by Caroline Langrishe.

The second blow concerned the budget, which had already been approved in principle by both CBS and the directors of Consolidated, who considered the amount would be judged fair by the corporation. We needed $900,000 per film, but now CBS was prepared to give us only $750,000. Take it or leave it. More of the familiar cost cutting. We had planned to do two shows on location in Malta. Forget it. Eventually Malcolm Burgess, remaining as our associate producer, Bill Launder (the accountant and another tower of strength), Clifton, and

I managed to force the overall price for five films down to around $4.25 million, still leaving us with a deficit of half a million. Deficits are more normal than not for a network show where the broadcaster simply buys a license to air the films for a limited amount of runs—thereafter the producing company has the right to syndicate it in America and sell to all other territories in the world (essentially the producer owns the production in perpetuity). Reasonable enough, and we were potentially covered because Radio Television Luxembourg had been persuaded by John Pringle to buy a stake in Consolidated and they needed product.

But we were still not through the hoop. John Whitney had stepped down as the chief of Capital Radio and recently taken on the full-time role of Consolidated's managing director. He is a very good man to work with and is a true friend—I still meet up with him today—however he wasn't happy about *QED*'s financial structure. A meeting was called at the studio and attended by Messrs. Whitney, Pringle, and Olswang, plus John Hawkesworth and me.

"Either you will work to a budget of $750,000 or I will instantly resign from the company," declared Whitney.

Bloody Hell! That was a toughie and a half—with icing. We absolutely did not want to see him leave, but . . .

"We simply can't do it for the price. Not if we are to give the production the gloss it needs," I said with the knowledge that the entire administrative team had shaved off every penny they could.

"Cut some corners," from someone at the table was not particularly helpful.

"Which ones?" I asked.

Silence.

"The only possible solution is for John Hawkesworth, Ron Austin, and Jim Buchanan to come up with new and less complex scripts."

Eager eyes swung to John.

"Yes," he said, "but starting all over again means we could never commence filming this year, which means CBS would probably pull out."

The debate was becoming unproductive.

"Look," I said as I trod onto dangerous ground. "Why don't you find another producer who says he can do it for the price you want? Whether he can or not is something we will see."

Coffee was finished quickly and the head-office brigade set off for London.

The following morning I remained in bed late; read the newspaper from cover to cover, drank copious amounts of coffee, and left the phone off the hook; and dealt with personal paperwork and generally tidied up my bachelor life. By now, for better or for worse, Caroline and I were separated, and my home-running chores had potentially increased somewhat. To give credit where it is due, a lovely woman who lived directly across the road from me had stepped into the housekeeping department. (Vi Donno was in her seventies and treated me like an adopted son, and she and her elderly husband made sure I was kept up to high domestic standards—cats fed, laundry done, food in the fridge and early morning wake-up calls when required.)

Lest I give a wrong impression about Caroline, I have to make it clear that she handled our departure on to different paths in life with great dignity and thoughtfulness. Shortly she was to marry her first love, David Anderson (son of director Michael), and they had a daughter together by the name of Holly—I've always wondered why "Holly." (Caroline, should you ever read this book, will you be kind enough to send me an e-mail with the answer—sorry, I keep forgetting to ask you when face-to-face!)

Eventually I arrived at the studio—must have been lunchtime.

"Where have you been?" Liz demanded of me.

I told her.

"They've been on the phone all morning."

"Oh, what did they have to say?" She gave me a "you know bloody well" look. "I'll get John Whitney on the line right now."

I must admit I was tempted to be a bit naughty and wander off to the parking lot while she dialed the number.

"We don't want another producer," said John.

"But I simply cannot make the planned series at the price you would like—it just can't be done."

He understood completely and told me Consolidated would come up with what was needed. It wasn't a climbdown on his part—it was the statement of a realist who trusted what I was telling him. For this I will ever respect him.

Third blow:

Malcolm Burgess: "We can't have Wembley Studios."

"Why ever not?"

Barbra Streisand had decided to make her directorial debut there at the same time, and *Yentl* needed all the stages.

Outrageous news: although we had been perfectly content at our first base, Twickenham Studios, it had been made clear in advance we could not be accommodated for our new five episodes because of a previous booking. So we had lined up Wembley.

Wembley Studios was owned by the Lee brothers—John and Benny. Originally they had been electricians who had built a powerful little empire, recently dragging Wembley out of rat-infested dereliction. The property had been built in the 1930s to house Twentieth Century-Fox's U.K. productions, which were known as "Quota Quickies"—the lawyer's method of overcoming Britain's limited import quota, especially from America. Subsequently it was taken over by Associated Redifusion for its burgeoning television output, but by the mid-1970s Wembley had become unused. John and Benny, along with their young studio manager Dennis Carrigan, had done a wonderful job of restoration, and an exciting future lay before them—not least having a Hollywood star like Streisand on their lot.

"Now what's all this about?" I asked Dennis over the telephone. "We have first refusal on the space, and Streisand or no, you guys have a moral obligation to honor it."

"But you've not made a firm booking; she has," he responded.

"Come on—you know the game."

"I'll get back to you," he concluded.

We were potentially snared—what with budget constraints and the like, we had genuinely been unable to make a final commitment to anyone about anything. "I've discussed it with John and Benny, and we think you're right," Dennis confessed the following day. "You have first refusal, and we'll hold the position. When can you confirm?"

"Two days at the most." The securing of deficit funding was nearly in place.

"Done."

"And what about *Yentl*?"

"They're happy to push back a few weeks."

Phew—England was busy at the time, and there was no other proper space available. God bless the Lee brothers and Dennis for their professionalism and loyalty. And, belatedly, thank you Miss Streisand.

Somehow or other we had fended off the blows, and so we continued with our preparations in sublime ignorance of the hardest blow of all that would hit *QED*.

One more trip to Los Angeles to tie up the final production details with CBS. Just three nights staying at my father's splendid home in Beverly Hills. On the second evening Sam's agent called to ask for a breakfast meeting the following morning.

Oh, Christ! I thought. "Is everything all right?"

"Everything's great, and Sam's looking forward to seeing you all in England next week."

I sighed in relief. Nevertheless, I entered the Polo Lounge at the Beverly Hills Hotel in some trepidation. In my experience a lot of Hollywood agents can throw spanners into the works. Although this might be because they are protecting their own patch, it is more likely they simply don't understand the cottage industry methods of filmmaking in Europe—or didn't then.

Actually I need not have worried; this agent couldn't have been more helpful—he simply wanted to ensure we were as happy with Sam as Sam was with us.

"Absolutely. Can I make one suggestion, though?"

"Go ahead."

"Should he have any concerns about anything at all, he should come and see me first rather than harboring a grief and having to wait until you are in your office to air it."

He was surprised.

"We can probably sort a matter out before the sun even rises in LA."

He thanked me and said he would tell his client just that.

Only once did Sam ever come to my office with a request. His wife Lynn was passing through London—just one night—and he asked if he might be released from the set a little earlier than our 7:00 P.M. norm. And of course he was. I mention this as a further example of how easy it was to work with our leading man.

I returned to England a happy chap and, believing the worst was behind us, was really looking forward to the commencement of principal photography.

But . . .

The schedule was for ten weeks (crossing over Christmas) and of mostly five working days each. This is more productive than the six-day week, which is pretty pointless unless away from base on overnight locations. And each film would be shot as an independent whole with its own director. The first was Don Sharp, the second Roy Ward Baker, the third Henry Herbert, followed by Don again and then Roy.

Because of the limited daylight hours, the plan was to shoot in the studio as much as possible—especially after Christmas, when the worst of the winter weather is apt to strike. However, it would have been hopeless to confine the show to interiors alone, so we took a gamble with the first episode—we had to. *The Great Motor Race* is precisely that. Deverill and his jet-powered car versus Kilkiss, who is promoting the Japanese motor industry—and cheating, naturally. Usually cars don't interest me remotely, but this one did. For the escape chase in the "pilot" we had had the kaiser's car specially built, as it was more than likely to end up a wreck. It was a Mark 10 Jaguar beneath the skin. Damage was minimal, and we could use it again for this new episode after fanciful redressing—rocket boosters and all. Many other less elaborate vehicles were also required, and Malcolm, an aficionado, collected together a superb array of vintage examples.

The race was due to commence on our second filming day—the first day being a kind of warm-up in the studio.

"We need a decision on the weather cover," said Clifton.

Weather cover is an alternative interior day's work in the event of inclemency. I had already told him I was the worst person to ask. Not that I was afraid of making decisions but because I usually got it wrong. If the forecast was for fair or good conditions, I would opt for going outside, and it would rain. The opposite applied. To break the pattern, I had even tried committing the crew to studio work when we were promised a sunny day—and the sun shone—and vice versa.

"So what do you want to do tomorrow, location or studio?" Clifton persisted.

"What does the Weather Centre say?"

"Sun."

"Better get out then, I guess, but don't be surprised if there's a downpour all day."

5:00 A.M. on the Tuesday morning . . .

Just as I went out to get in my car, a flurry of powdery snow gently brushed the windshield. It was too early in the winter for it to be serious—a thaw by midmorning was most likely. Boy, how wrong I was!

My car was a four-wheel drive, and all four were needed as I began to struggle through thicker and thicker snow toward the location, which was about an hour north of London. I got there at around 8:30, and, remarkably, so did most other members of the cast and crew. But it was hopeless—no car racing for sure. Fortunately there were a couple of scenes that could be switched from exterior to interior and shot on the site, so the crew was able to carry on with those for a while. By 10:30 everyone finally made it to the location (bar one person whose car had been trapped in the snow and the train he took as an alternative method of transport got itself iced up in a tunnel). This was actually much, much more than remarkable because by noon England was all but shut down. Roads closed by ever-increasing snowdrifts or accidents—the same with railways—power cuts—airports inoperative—just about nothing was functioning. Except the amazing *QED* unit.

Midday back at the studio to make a damage assessment and to look at how we would proceed for the remainder of the week if no thaw came.

"We have insurance for this don't we?" asked John Whitney over the phone.

"No . . ."

"Why not?"

"It's exceptionally rare for a film to carry weather insurance—the cost is prohibitive."

He informed me he would check this out with some brokers he knew but never came back to me on the matter, so I guess they had confirmed what I had told him.

Back to the future. Certainly we could keep going in the studio for another four days, but by the next Tuesday we would be deep in something very unpleasant. Consequently it was essential for the crew to be outside whenever remotely possible.

By Thursday the conditions eased slightly and on the Friday of the first week the car race was finally started. This now left us with studio weather cover until the Tuesday night. The situation was desperate, but not serious.

Act prudently and put everyone on standby to begin Roy Baker's episode earlier than planned. At least Deverill's house interior was a "standing set," and we could work with the ongoing principals.

The blizzard returned for the weekend; however, we did manage to get out on the following Wednesday. But the next day was worse than ever. So Roy's episode went into production. The exteriors for this one were not as demanding in terms of weather as for Don's, but we still got hit.

By now I had to invoke an infrequently used clause in the Equity agreement—force majeure. This meant all the actors (other than the running cast) on *The Great Motor Race* had their contracts suspended. The union bleated about this.

"You can't do it," averred an official at a conciliation meeting. (By this time Equity and the BFTPA were talking to each other again.)

"I believe I can. The blizzard is not in our control."

"Production should not have been started in the winter," he pressed.

"No choice because of delivery dates to CBS."

Not for a moment did I really think we would get away with it, but had I not made the attempt, I would have been failing in my duties. There was no conclusive outcome from the meeting; however, Equity remained silent on the matter thereafter—until the next time I tried similar tactics.

And so the pattern continued with Clifton and me trying to keep one step ahead—even the unit's short Christmas break was marred except for it being a genuine white one.

Received a card from Caroline—she and David were in Sydney. "Do write and tell me how *QED* is going."

In my letter back I said, "It's a bit like balancing on a tightrope when blindfolded and trying to juggle bars of soap in a rainstorm."

Henry's film, *4:10 to Zurich*, started a week ahead of schedule, and still the first two shows were incomplete, but at least we hadn't lost a day's work—yet.

Things picked up a bit at the Deverill house exterior location. All three directors shared the cast and crew over one day—really quite funny.

One scene had Deverill and his team being taken into some woods to be killed by a scheming, gun-loose woman in the employ of Kilkiss, who had got his hands on a chemical weapon of mass destruction. The area was by now completely free of snow. That should have been good, but it led to another difficulty the very same week.

The unit traveled to Norfolk for three overnights while filming on the Nene Valley Railway. And would you "Adam and Eve it"? (Cockney rhyming slang for "believe it.") Back came the bloody blizzard with a vengeance.

The fields alongside the railway track were a blanket of white as far as the eye could see, and the chill factor, when shooting outside on a moving train, was nothing short of arctic. But on went the crew, never missing a beat.

"What are you going to do about the capture scene?" said Sam over dinner on our first evening.

He was asking how it would be possible to shoot the moments when he and the others are forcibly taken off the train before being led into the snow-free woods at gunpoint.

"If I had the answer," I told him, "I wouldn't be standing around in the ice of Norfolk, I'd be sitting at the side of God the Father Almighty."

He laughed—in fact we all laughed. The whole situation was ludicrous beyond belief.

As Henry and I traveled by car to the location the next morning, we spotted something quite extraordinary. On the right-hand side of the road was a wood standing on a hill amidst the brown of last year's fallen leaves—not a trace of snow. To the left the ground sloped away to the valley, which was still as white as it could be.

All we needed was one shot of our group with the snowy background and pan with them into the wood before cutting to the scene we had already completed. So off I went at lunchtime with a small second unit and the principal actors.

Sam decided it was time to have some fun with me as the "director for an hour." He leads the group with the others a few paces behind, and behind them is the lady with the gun. The actress, Elizabeth Shepherd, is not particularly tall, and, being hampered by boots with highish heels, along with trampling through the mushy leaves, she simply could not keep up with her captives, who could have made good their escape with ease.

"Cut . . . Sam will you walk a little slower, please."

"Sure . . ."

Take two and he did walk a little slower—a very little bit slower.

"Cut . . ."

It was all very funny—made the more so, I suspect, because we felt we were out of the woods with the weather (unfortunate pun!). Six takes it took for him to go slowly enough, by which time my tears of laughter had turned to icicles. What better way to spend a lunch hour?

At the risk of repeating myself, the key to remaining on budget is to remain on schedule at almost any cost. (To prove it by reverse example, see our experiences on *Bellman and True* in chapter 6.)

With his first episode at last completed, Don Sharp was able to concentrate on his next, *To Catch a Ghost*. This story concerned Deverill's exposure of financial malpractices with ghosts as red herrings. Quite a number of special effects were needed, which can be very time consuming, exacerbated when working with principal actors in the same shot. Consequently it was hardly surprising that by the second week of shooting, the schedule had slipped by a day.

There was only one thing for it. Bring in a small second unit with me as the unpaid director. A lot of little bits needed clearing up, but there was also a scene to be shot with Sam, AC, and George Innes in a church. These three could be released from work at Wembley Studios until 1:00 P.M. It was going to be tight.

The plan was to walk through the action and dialogue and then work it out setup by setup—ten shots in all. Cameraman Jimmy Devis was then given up to two hours to light the church for every angle, and once we started, each shot would have to be completed within the space of ten minutes.

While Jim was getting on with the preparations, I took myself off to our temporary greenroom.

Sitting there was a very pretty blonde-haired girl who had been taken on for the day. Sally-Ann Abel, later to become Sally-Ann Neame, was the unit nurse. We chatted for an hour or so and found we had quite a lot in common. The divorced mother of four (I had three children by my first marriage) and much more recently separated from her boyfriend (as I was from Caroline), her sparkling personality was instantly engaging.

The evening of the penultimate day. Caroline Langrishe's agent on the telephone:

"She's pretty unwell . . . flu with a temperature of 104 . . . can't even stand up."

Poor, love. But never mind—insurance claim for the nonappearance of an actor on grounds of ill health. A light Friday for everyone else as we did a bit of pickup shots. And after the weekend her final sequence was in the can within a few hours.

With a large number of "unavoidable blows" behind us, we could at last take life at a less frantic pace—and we were smack on budget. John Whitney was the first to come and give everyone a warm hug.

There was still work to be done though: editing, music scoring (Howard and Blaikley again), and John Hawkesworth and Ron and Jim had to start thinking about another twenty-two adventures for Quentin Everhard Deverill.

"You know," said John. "I have to admit there's a side of me that hopes we are not 'picked up.' I can't see how we could ever do it."

Privately I had to agree with him. Filming in the United Kingdom is very much a pioneering process every time, and we just didn't have studios like Paramount or Universal—places offering a factory-like environment where so much material can be shot on the lot. Speed was an essential if we were to stick by the American actors' period of time off the series per year. And for sure we didn't have the Californian weather. Turning a blind eye, I said, "We'll do it somehow." A "closet show"— one in five set in a shoe-cupboard and filmed in five days. I don't know.

"I've just received this memo for you from CBS," remarked Liz. "And I've no idea what it means."

Three and three-quarter columns of recipient names, ten down, and mine at the very bottom on the right. It read:

Target: London—23rd March 1982—8:00 P.M.

"Haven't a clue," I responded. "Obviously to do with network scheduling." And that prompted an idea. We sent a memo back to all thirty-seven people listing our grand total of six episodes by title in the order we wished them to be aired. Extraordinary, that's exactly what happened. It bears out a theory—when working with conglomerates consider the fact that no one wants to appear less informed than the next person, so simply tell them "what is what," and they'll all follow like sheep. Apology to Alan Wagner due here—his name wasn't on the list, and I never told him what I did!

What a shame Concorde is no longer available for flights to Washington—pure state of the art of aviation. What grace and what punch, something like a thoroughbred racehorse all but knocking the wind out of the rider. I flew on one for the CBS press screenings for their new shows at the Watergate Hotel (among them *Cagney and Lacey*). Sam was in attendance too. There were two rooms full of eager journalists, and very nearly all were friendly enough—though most of them wanted to quiz Sam about *Heaven's Gate* and Michael Cimino.

As we entered the second room, Sam whispered to me, "Watch out for the old woman on the far side of the table. She's a wolf in sheep's clothing."

And so she proved, having bided her time.

Petite, sixties with gray hair piled up on her head and secured by what looked like two knitting needles—a perfect cartoon granny-witch. Slowly her eyes settled on me.

"*Mis-turr* Neame," she said in a menacing voice. "Hasn't all this kind of thing been done before?"

They had just viewed *Target: London* and Kilkiss's attempts to bomb the city with his missile. Luckily a response came to me instantly. "You mean by filmmakers or the Germans?"

Hoots of laughter from all around, and the poor woman sank without trace.

Postscript

March 23, 1982—and the first of the *QED* films aired across the United States as scheduled. The ratings were pretty good but just not quite up there. Unhappily it had been pitched against powerful and already proven Monday night shows on ABC and NBC. Figures climbed for the second week, though not by enough, and by the third it was clear we were not going to make it in the network world. I think three things were against us—the show was not set in the more familiar American locations—it was a period subject (vastly more suited to PBS)—and was either behind or ahead of its time. By that I mean it could have fallen into the successful spoof type of production like Vincent Price's *The Abominable Dr. Phibes* of the early 1970s or the dark world of *Harry Potter* today. But genre comparisons are a complete waste of time and prove nothing.

Simon Olswang and John Pringle secured a leaseback deal that let Radio Television Luxembourg off the hook for its deficit funding, and a sale was made to London Weekend Television. For some reason, best known to schedulers, it was transmitted only within the company's footprint over southeastern England and even then early on Sunday afternoons. True or false, we couldn't help feeling we were being taught a lesson: don't step out of your own patch.

Anyway, everyone who was involved in making or appearing in *QED* remembers it very fondly as a great (albeit tough) experience and as a good production. The episodic guest actors—English and U.S. residents—gave of their very best and were equal to any to be seen on mainstream American TV—yes, the North American arm of Equity got a fair look in too. ·

By the summer of 1982, Sally-Ann and I had started a relationship (that happily survives today), and we were in America taking a short trip through Arizona—Williams was one port of call for a night. After dinner we got to talking with a couple of waitresses in a desert diner. S-A supplied the reply when asked about what I did.

"Oh, wow! You made *QED*. The best show we've had on TV for years." And both seemed to know every story line and every character. "Don't you just love, Quentin."

Useless bit of information—the series is also known as Mastermind.

CHAPTER FOUR

Blarney

A hyena leapt off the ground and landed in Viv Bristow's arms.

"He just wants the attention," said Viv, a tall and good-looking farmer in Zimbabwe, who had an orphanage for wild animals. "And he thinks he's a lion."

This particular hyena shared a large pen with a big cat who was a bit docile that day because he had been bitten on the nose by a puff adder.

It was necessary for them to be caged because once having been rescued (perhaps after running amok where they shouldn't have), these animals soon lost the ability to fend for themselves in the African bush—they would have been rejected by their own kind and probably slaughtered.

John Hawkesworth and I were back in Africa in 1982 to look into the possibility of making a series from *Jock of the Bushveldt* for Consolidated, and it was a subject requiring even more animal actors than we had had on *Flame Trees*. The trip through South Africa's Eastern Transvaal, traversing the Drakensberg Mountains, was wonderful—not that one could ever escape the appalling apartheid business. Then north to Harare and into the rugged terrain to meet with Viv. His communication skills with the wildlife were out on their own. The African elephant is not known for its gregariousness, and in fact one is best advised to keep well out of its way. But there was this man walking freely in the veldt calling a matriarch by name, and before long she appeared at the head of half a dozen of the creatures with their dangerous tusks curving upward just above the ground—each in turn nuzzling Viv with their trunks as they flapped their jumbo-sized ears. We were very excited and knew we were destined to get some astonishing footage. Except we weren't. In spite of the efforts of all at Consolidated, funding could not be secured.

By this time the company was expanding—more permanent staff being employed—grand new premises on the edge of Central London's Regent's Park—and ambitious plans. I was never to work with them again, which did not sadden me as it had somehow lost the charm of the old intimate "family" days. Hawkesworth was to do a couple more shows under its banner for the BBC (four-camera video in the studio). Shortly, John Whitney was to leave to become head of the Independent Broadcasting Authority, and someone else was brought in in his place. Consolidated grew rapidly, perhaps too rapidly for its own good and by the late 1980s had offices in the United Kingdom and United States. Then suddenly it imploded. I've no idea what happened and am only thankful I had sold my shares at the start of its blooming days.

James Mitchell and I had initially met when he was Kenneth Tynan's lawyer. Since then he had formed a TV film company called Little Bird (his nickname for his wife Jane) and set up shop in Ireland. The first production he made was six episodes for the United Kingdom's new Channel Four based on the short stories by Sommerville and Ross—*The Irish RM*. He was now intent on setting up an entirely different series, and with a commission for another six *RMs*, he needed someone to produce them.

Bit odd, if you think about it, I always seemed to be involved with shows known by their initials—*UXB*, *QED*—and now this, meaning "Resident Magistrate." And, oh, boy it was set just before World War I! Ireland was still under British control then and these largely ex-army officers and, more often than not, unqualified magistrates were posted around the country to keep law and order—attempt to anyway, as it was a nation of people who were a law unto themselves—poaching, smuggling, making poteen (moonshine), wenching, and generally causing mischief. But as everyone knows the majority of the Irish are as lovable and soft as their accents.

There were some splendid characters—Bryan Murray as "Flurry Knox," whose enthusiasm for "the chase" outweighs most everything else; Niall Toibin, ever the crafty "Slipper"; and Anna Manahan playing the housekeeper, Mrs. Cadogan, which she demanded be pronounced "Kay-der-gorne."

The only tricky thing was having a protagonist, who in the books is the "I" character. It tends to make them an observer without being a fully rounded character. Peter Bowles handled the difficulty extremely well, creating a sympathetic Major Sinclair Yeates, who frequently finds himself drawn into unfitting situations.

It was fortunate that the old team could be brought together again. Malcolm Burgess with his painstaking mind for budgetary detail and logic in general, Clifton Brandon with his equally precise handling of schedules, and Liz Bunton to keep us under some sort of overall control—we were still in the days when practical jokes at work were not frowned upon! A fun-loving young woman herself, she has a fetching laugh and a warm welcome for everyone while, at the same time, possessing the built-in discipline of a well-educated English lady (true, her language had its riper moments). Since pre-*UXB* days she had been a tireless student of the realities of production and at twenty-seven was barely a few steps from taking on a senior role. I was lucky she didn't move up before we had the chance of working together one last time. What makes her all the more special is her attractiveness and complete femininity—something that, when used wisely, can enhance a leadership quality.

And along came a favored camera operator who I must have known for at least twenty-five years—Geoff Glover.

There were also two other extraordinary (under the circumstances) additions to the crew coming to Ireland from England—my ex-wife, Caroline, working as Malcolm's assistant, and her husband, David. He is an exceptionally able assistant director, and this was not to be the only production we would do together. Guess the arrangement sounds a bit bizarre, but it was all right—and Sally-Ann was on location with us as well.

The first thing Clifton and I had done in preparation was to screen the original six episodes. In our opinion the show needed tightening up and shaping and had to be far slicker. In hindsight, I'm not altogether sure this was right.

Scripts were got under way, and the usual struggles with budgets were slowly overcome—around £300,000 per hour as opposed to our previous year's production of $850,000 (or say somewhere a bit over £500,000). But at least we were not dealing with the U.S. network demands—particularly when it came to option contracts with the actors.

Late summer was soon upon us, and we had to complete filming in Ireland before Christmas (and, God forbid, more snow), which meant that principal photography had to commence by no later than the start of October. But we had no director.

Originally I had approached Lionel Jeffries, better known as an actor. He played Grandpa Potts (at the age of forty-one) in *Chitty Chitty Bang Bang* and King Pellinore in the magnificent *Camelot* plus hundreds of other parts over the years. He is less remembered as a director, although his debut with *The Railway Children* is a very good piece of work. He was keen to do the *RM* films, and Peter Bowles was equally keen for him to join us. In the end, he was unable to wait for our financial negotiations to be concluded with Channel Four and went on tour with the female impersonator Danny La Rue (actors have to earn the rent like everyone else).

Eventually Peter Sykes saved the day—we had done a Hammer horror film together ten years before—by taking a sabbatical from his current employment as a lecturer in film at a university. He was to do three episodes, and the indefatigable Roy Baker was lined up for the other three.

Ultimately it was a straightforward production, and it is pointless me waffling on here about situations without some sort of adventure for the reader, so I'll confine myself to just one thing. Earlier in these pages I mentioned that having one's back against the wall makes for greater creativity. Here's a nice example.

A story line called for a merchant ship to be wrecked off the Irish coast during a stormy night, and, rather as in *Whiskey Galore*, its alcoholic cargo gets swept up onto the beach by dawn. This was precomputer imaging and would cost so much to create properly that the only sensible choice was to ditch the episode in favor of something more manageable. Yet there had to be a way.

Okay, make it a dawn sequence (so it could be shot during the day—blue filter on the camera and underexposed emulsion so not too much

War-torn London 1943? No—street demolition. *Danger U.X.B.*, 1978. Copyright Thames Television 1978.

"Lieutenant Ash" (Anthony Andrews) and his squad of "sappers"—all of them fine actors. They usually did not sit at the same table as the "officer" actors during meal breaks! Copyright Thames Television 1978.

Anthony Andrews preparing for the scene when he is blown off the pier. I watch on as Judy Geeson does something to Tony's shoes. From the author's private collection.

"Ash," assisted by his "sergeant" (Maurice Roëves), defuses a fiberglass bomb. Copyright Thames Television 1978.

Tony, Judy, John Hawkesworth, and I try rolling an even larger bomb. Copyright Thames Television 1978.

Director Bob Brooks (left) steers the Steadicam operator. Actor Michael Elphick (as one of the "Knowledge Boys") is at center bottom. *The Knowledge,* 1979. Copyright Thames Television 1979.

Elspeth Huxley visits the location in Kenya. The girl behind her was Holly Aird's double—she was the more secure rider! *The Flame Trees of Thika,* 1980. Copyright Thames Television 1980.

Filming outside the house built by Roy Stannard. Luckily it did not burn down. Courtesy Ian Wilson.

Hayley Mills as "Elspeth's" mother "Tilly." A character of great strength. Copyright Thames Television 1980.

John Hawkesworth puffs on a pungent cigar as he sketches some Masai warriors. Copyright Thames Television 1980.

Hawkesworth and me. Copyright Thames Television 1980.

Imported rain. Courtesy Ian Wilson.

Cameraman Ian Wilson looking as if he has set up another prank. Courtesy Ian Wilson.

Me, Elspeth, Roy Ward Baker, and Malcolm Burgess. Copyright Thames Television 1980.

Holly, by now friends with "Moyale" the pony. Copyright Thames Television 1980.

The wagon drawn by oxen at Lewa Downs. Courtesy Ian Wilson.

Henry Herbert, 17th Earl of Pembroke.
Courtesy the Wilton Estate.

Verity Lambert wisely wears a solar topee against the Kenyan sun. I don't remember being cross about anything! Copyright Thames Television 1980.

Sam Waterston (Deverill) demonstrates the theory of television. Circa 1912. Q.E.D., 1981. From the author's private collection.

Sam chats to my father during a visit to Wembley Studios. Ronnie had directed him in *Hopscotch* two years earlier. From the author's private collection.

A. C. Weary on the left, Sarah Berger, Sam, and Richard Morant. They are temporarily "detained" by the rotten "Kilkiss." From the author's private collection.

Deverill with Phipps (George Innes) posing in Uhlan uniform—pickelhaube and all. See the second picture in this photo spread, with George at far right. From the author's private collection.

Liz Bunton (left) and script assistant Juliet Clarke. Note the Edwardian advertisement for spirits—thanks to some wag in the Art Department! Courtesy Liz Bunton.

Peter Bowles and friend. *The Irish R.M.*, 1983. Courtesy Little Bird.

Father Quixote (Alec Guinness) and "Sancho" (Leo McKern) discuss the Holy Trinity beneath some graffiti. *Monsignor Quixote*, 1985. Copyright Thames Television 1985.

Leo McKern, Rodney Bennett, Graham Greene and Alec Guinness in Spain. Copyright Thames Television 1985.

Johnny Goodman and Muir Sutherland on the location. Copyright Thames Television 1985.

Richard Loncraine (left) behind a very long camera and lens. *Bellman and True*, 1985. Copyright Thames Television 1987.

Jack Rosenthal—*The Knowledge*, 1979, and *Bye, Bye, Baby*, 1991. Courtesy Jack Rosenthal.

Goofing around the camera on the set of *Soldier Soldier*, 1993. Clockwise from left, Robson Green with clapper board, Gary Love with light meter, Jerome Flynn on the operator's seat, and fellow actor Akim Mogaji. Courtesy Frank Elliott.

Sally-Ann and me on our wedding day in 1991. From the author's private collection.

A foray into musical theater. *The Courtenay* Ensemble, 2003. Courtesy Bright Start Productions.

detail could be taken in by the viewer) and set it after the violence of the storm has abated—no (famously) waiting endlessly for tempest conditions in Ireland as had David Lean on *Ryan's Daughter*.

Without visual reference placed alongside a line of rocks in the sea (a standing man, for example), the two-dimensional eye of the camera will not reveal their actual size. Similarly, use a scaled-down vessel, which need only be two-dimensional itself, or perhaps give it a little depth for overall shape. Finally run the camera at a speed relative to the size of the miniature. Designer Roy Stannard's hull was thirty feet in length, which was around a third of the length of a nineteenth-century cargo ship—so once positioned on the rocks, with the camera shooting at seventy-five frames a second (slow motion), the real waves rolling past it would create the illusion of a full-sized ship. Add to this three upright poles for masts and attach some canvas on crossbeams—with a slight breeze, these mock-up sails would flap in slow motion too. So far so good. But why not go for gold and include actors and a couple of words of dialogue? Filmed at normal speed, of course.

We schedule a day for shooting the scene when the tide would be right out in the morning, and while the filming unit carried on with other work, Roy and his team placed the miniature on the rocks and anchored it down. The sea level would rise to a visually correct height by 1:08 P.M., and everyone needed to be ready to get the shot in the can by no later than 1:14, when our ship would most likely be swept away.

Everything was readied in good time. A horse-drawn wagon with Major Yeates and Flurry Knox aboard, with others on either side of it— all out to try and help the wrecked seamen. On "Action!" it would trundle up a slope— someone points, "There she is!" and the camera would pan to our ship.

1:05 P.M.—Tension was mounting amongst the unit.

1:07—Silence but for the lapping waves and a slight breeze.

1:08—Not there yet.

God, this entire episode was dependent on the scene working. What if it didn't?

1:10—Still not right. Support scaffolding and daylight visible beneath the hull.

1:12—Nearly . . .

Snap . . .

Something gave way.

Instantly our construction manager and his team were in the water.

Planking had come off the hull's frame.

1:13—Hammers, nails. . . . Anything.

1:14—Still not secured.

Three more minutes passed.

"Will it hold?" I asked Roy.

"Let's hope."

1:20—It should all be over . . .

Two minutes more . . .

Finally . . .

"Action!" called Peter Sykes.

And the wagon started up the hill with the camera initially running at the standard twenty-five frames per second.

Meanwhile the stalwart construction boys were swimming out of shot as quickly as they could—no matter if they didn't make it in time, I thought, they'll look like sailors abandoning ship.

A pointed hand from one actor beside the wagon, and "There she is!" he cried in full voice.

Camera operator Geoff Glover panned the camera seaward—increasing the speed of the pan as he went. Cameraman Jack Conroy opened the lens aperture (no shutter angle adjustment on our Arriflex) to compensate for exposure as his assistant wound up the camera's speed to seventy-five frames. Talk about teamwork.

1:23—"Cut!"

And within moments our vessel was eased off the rocks by the rising sea and gently turned turtle.

It was one of those heart-warming occasions when everyone applauded each other.

Just had to hope our adventurous timing of waves, exposure, panning, and camera speed was right and the laboratories back in London didn't graunch the footage when processing it that night.

8:00 A.M. the next morning—"You got it," said our editor after viewing the rushes in London. "Terrific. Well done to you all."

The Irish RM was well liked (both in the United Kingdom and on PBS in the United States), but I quickly came to the conclusion I had been wrong to zip it up. The undulating simplicity of the first series had been truer to the authors' original concept and truer to the Irish people as a whole—obviously the demands of network TV were still running through my veins.

While working on a book like this, I tend to check out my memory on IMDB. It's a very useful reference tool although, as noted earlier, unavoidably prone to some inaccuracy. The thought of trying to change what's wrong to right on my own entry is not worth the hassle even though history could be better served. Besides, who will believe me when I say there were eighteen films in the series and not the twelve as claimed on the website—our six episodes have obviously gone AWOL!

James Mitchell invited me to make the third batch (ordered on the back of the second), but I declined with some regret, as I felt I had no more to offer—for the avoidance of doubt, as lawyers say, I was not in some petulant kind of a sulk! I enjoyed myself immensely—found the Irish a dream to work with and Peter Bowles a warm professional through and through. Yet I needed a new challenge; otherwise, there was a danger of earning the epithet "Ol' feet on the ground."

"Praise be to God," as Mrs. Cadogan might have exclaimed—something unexpected and very exciting lay just around the corner.

Postscript

My father has always enjoyed a drink, and he can hold it well. In fact at a celebration for him by BAFTA LA on his ninetieth birthday, he told the gathering, "Doctors have said to me throughout the years, 'Ronnie, if only you would drink a little less.' He went on to add, "They're all dead now!"

Christmas 1983 was spent with him in Los Angeles, and I brought him a bottle of poteen (heavily labeled, by me, with a skull and crossbones). It was an end of production gift from—s'pose I should not name anyone as the Garda might get on the case!

For a good fifteen years it remained unopened at the back of his bar before being chucked out (I think). Very wise.

CHAPTER FIVE

~

Tilting at Windmills

It came about like this:

"Got this series we want you to produce," said Johnny Goodman over at Euston Films. "Six-part thriller set in the East End (of London). Are you up for it?"

Already my heart had sunk—I was only in my early forties but was still wondering why my peers were working on tropical locations while I lumbered about in upper Europe. A non–period show had appeal, but gangsters and their molls didn't, even though anything with Verity Lambert's stamp on it was bound to be a class act. Thing was, though, Verity had recently left the Euston/Thames stable to pursue a career in cinema.

I declined Johnny's offer.

"Become a bit choosy, have you?" he said not unkindly—Johnny is not an unkind man.

"No," I replied. "It's just that I need to do something different, I need a challenge."

Four weeks went by.

Johnny called. "So how about this? Graham Greene novel . . ."

"Go on." My mind was alert.

"One-off film—set in Spain."

And I wanted to cry out, "Yeahhhh!"

"Two guys driving around the place and debating life."

"Johnny, now you're talking."

At least he was beginning to.

He sent the novel round by bike, and I sat down to read it. I don't think I have ever read anything so quickly in my life. That evening Sally-Ann returned from work to the house where we now lived in Kensington, and I spent far longer telling her about the project than it took me to read.

A couple of days later I met up with Johnny and Lloyd Shirley, who had taken over the reins from Verity, a position he had held once before—in fact, Lloyd was one of the founders of Euston Films.

I got the impression they were not overly keen on *Monsignor Quixote*, although neither said as much. It was Muir Sutherland who was the one behind it. Muir (a Hispanophile with a second home near Madrid) was director of programs at Thames and was "number two" to the managing director—the powerful and very bright Bryan (Ginger) Cowgill.

"We want you to go out on a survey to Spain as soon as possible," said Lloyd.

"Spend as long as you need there and," Johnny added generously, "take Sally-Ann along with you." This was not the last time he made such a suggestion.

"But first read the screenplay," said Lloyd. "Excellent writer . . . Peter Luke. But Graham Greene has script approval and he doesn't like it. What you'll have to try and do is convince him it's okay."

Wonderful!

The truth of the matter is Greene was absolutely right. The script was pretty bad and bore little relationship to his fabulous novel. Frankly I wasn't prepared to produce a film from it and certainly had no intention of trying to convince the eminent author of its merits.

Initially I was vetted by his brother Hugh Carlton-Greene, who earlier had been the director general of the BBC (many say the best there ever was). I seemed to pass muster and three days later was ushered into a modest bedroom at London's Ritz Hotel—the novelist's base when over from his home in Antibes in the south of France.

His reputation was awesome in the best sense, plus he was known for chewing up filmmakers for breakfast. Physically, the most striking thing about Greene were his eyes—a delicate shade of blue and unquestionably those retained from a mischievous childhood. He rose from a chair by the window to greet me—a tall man with head slightly bowed.

After the normal pleasantries were done, he looked at me almost accusingly.

"Well what do you think about the script for *Monsignor Quixote?*"

"It's no good."

Instantly he seemed to relax.

"You know I have script approval?" he stated.

"Yes."

"I can't think how I got it. My agent, Pollinger, asked and Thames agreed," he said humbly before adding, "I've never had it before."

He wanted to know how I would go about getting the script right.

"Start from scratch—go back to the book."

"I've made a list of the important scenes we should keep."

"Better if we could keep the lot," I said.

"You think you can—in two hours of screen time?"

"I'll do my best."

The survey in Spain was scheduled for the next week, and he suggested I meet up with his traveling companion Father Leopoldo Durán, a professor of English at the University of Madrid. Apparently, on many occasions, Greene and the priest had driven around Spain visiting almost every place of interest—actually they didn't drive themselves, as neither could; the car they rented was in the hands of someone more capable who they amusingly called "The Third Man."

Quixote was born during these journeys, and the two principal characters are based on a mixture of them both.

"Father Quixote" is the parish priest of the small town of El Toboso in La Mancha. One day he goes to the help of a bishop from Rome, on his way to Madrid on papal business, who has run out of petrol. The bishop takes a shine to Quixote and tells him he would like to see him traveling the highways in the name of God and chivalry as did his fictitious forebear. Within a matter of weeks the priest learns that the Holy Father, himself, has appointed him to the rank of monsignor, and consequently he will lose his parish. Meanwhile the Communist mayor of El Toboso, Zancas, is voted out of office, and the two men find they have something in common—no position in their town. So they decide to take a roving holiday around Spain in the monsignor's red car, which he calls "Rocinante" after the original Quixote's knackered horse. They take with them a good supply of wine and stop to drink it here and there along the way. While driving and relaxing they debate the apparently opposing benefits or otherwise of Communism and the Church. There are some delightfully funny exchanges. On their first evening picnic, Monsignor Quixote tries to explain to "Sancho"—a nickname he bestows on Zancas (as in Sancho Panza)—about the Holy Trinity. By way of example he picks up two of their empty bottles.

> QUIXOTE: *The wine they contained was of the same substance and born at the same time. There you have God, the Father and God, the Son and . . .* (He moves a third—half—bottle forward) *and here, God, the Holy Ghost. Same substance, same birth. They're inseparable. Whoever partakes of one partakes of all three.*
> SANCHO: *The Holy Ghost has always seemed a bit redundant to me.*
> QUIXOTE: *We were not satisfied with two bottles, were we? That half bottle gives us that extra spark of life we both need. We wouldn't be so happy without it.*
> SANCHO: *You are very ingenious, friend. At least I understand what you mean by the Holy Trinity.*

Suddenly Quixote bows his head listlessly.

> SANCHO: *What's the matter, father?*
> QUIXOTE: *May God forgive me, for I have sinned. I think perhaps I am unworthy to be a priest.*
> SANCHO: *What have you done?*
> QUIXOTE: *I have given wrong instruction.*
> SANCHO: *Why?*
> QUIXOTE: *The Holy Ghost is equal in all respects to the Father and the Son and I have represented Him by a half bottle.*
> SANCHO (stands up): *Don't worry, father. The matter is easily put right.* (He picks up the half bottle and chucks it away) *I'll fetch a full bottle from the car and we'll still arrive safely in Madrid.*

(The above scene is reproduced here with the kind permission of David Higham Associates Ltd.)

As they journey on, they meet with various adventures that are modern parallels to some of the incidents in Cervantes' great book. And, like his "ancestor," many of the people he comes across think the monsignor is mad because of the odd situations his friend seems to get him into.

Sancho, who constantly believes the Guardia Civil are keeping him under surveillance (because he's a Communist), checks them into a private hotel where presentation of their identity papers would not be requested. A pretty waitress brings champagne to their room and gives Quixote a very sweet smile. The priest is delighted to see they must also cater for children, as there is a balloon beside the bed. He blows it up, and it bursts. It's actually a condom, and they are staying in a brothel.

Cinemas used to be a no-go area for the priesthood without special permission from a bishop, but by the time of our story, the rules were more liberal. Sancho takes Quixote to a film of the latter's choice—it is called "The Virgin's Prayer," a porno movie, naturally, with a misleading title. As they leave he says, "Oh, so that's how it's done. I'd always imagined it would be a great deal simpler and more enjoyable. They appeared to suffer rather a lot, judging from the sounds they made."

A passerby spots him and is astonished to see someone wearing a Roman collar coming out of such a film. Soon word (and a description) gets back to the bishop, under whom Quixote directly serves, and he is forcibly returned to El Toboso, there to be confined to his house. As further punishment for the incident and for earlier misunderstood situations, he is forbidden to say mass, even in private—a devastating thing for a man of his calling.

Sancho helps him make good his escape in Rocinante—now painted from red to blue to avoid any connection with Communism—and they start off on their second journey and its fatal conclusion.

Although lightheartedly written, as *an entertainment*, Greene continues the pair's discussions on theology and politics on a serious plain as well, but without the reader being aware of it. Another element of the piece is the growing affection of the two men for one another and their mutual respect for their chosen beliefs.

Sally-Ann and I met up with Father Durán, who turned out to be a man clearly enjoying life—not least his food and wine. He laughed a lot, told jokes, and spoke English at high speed, but still with a thickish accent. "Gosh!" was a frequently used word and pronounced "Hosh!" Fortunately he was able to join us on a four-day run over Father Quixote and Sancho's route. What a wonderful time. It was another occasion of going abroad for a working holiday with all expenses paid as well as money in the bank.

First the dusty red tracks of La Mancha overlooked by mesas, many with windmills on them. They really did look like the giants Cervantes describes. Madrid and its sophistication—El Prado—lovely buildings and excellent restaurants.

Then an hour to the west we caught site of the massive cross of *Valle de Los Caidos* (Valley of the Fallen). This soars above a church built into the rocks, the whole being a monument to those on both sides who died during Spain's civil war. Actually it looks more like a shrine to the dictator Franco and the entrance a monument to Fascist architecture. We would have to do a scene inside, right by Franco's tomb near the altar. No movie cameras had ever been allowed in there, so it was a bridge we would have to cross in due course. Horrid place.

On up through Salamanca, a beautiful city and the country's main seat of education; Valladolid, and on to León with its superb cathedral— the stained-glass windows a close second to those at Chartres; Osera in Galicia, and the monastery where the end of the story takes place.

Trappists are a silent order, but the monks are permitted to talk to guests, and boy! did they talk to us. And they made a special effort with the dinner because, in the novel, there is a comment about the food there not being very good.

After Quixote has been rescued from his confinement by Sancho, the two head for Galicia. The former feels wronged by his outraged and unforgiving bishop, and now he is no longer allowed to say mass; he believes himself merely a titular priest—not a proper priest anymore.

Their travels take them to a small town on its feast day, and there, being carried on a kind of bier from the church, is a statue of the Virgin Mary. Her clothes have money pinned all over them—money for the pocket of the local priest. Whoever puts up the most gets the best seat at the festivities, and everyone is eager to have their moment of importance. This was/is a common practice all over Galicia, but Quixote is horrified by the grotesque exhibition.

Furiously he confronts the priest. "It would be better to carry her through the streets naked."

What follows is a bit of quixotic chivalry. Sancho tries to pull the incensed monsignor away as he starts tearing the bank notes off the clothes. A riot breaks out with those for the ceremony versus those against.

Finally Sancho succeeds, and they take to their heels in Rocinante, hotly pursued by the Guardia Civil. They plan to take refuge in the nearby Trappist monastery, but just as they arrive there, Quixote loses control of the speeding car and crashes into a wall. Outwardly he appears severely concussed, although the injuries he has sustained are actually worse than that. The monks take him to a room and put him to bed, with his dear friend watching over him. During the night, he stirs and then rises like a sleepwalker and makes his way to the church—Sancho and the Superior following, not daring to wake him. Once in the church, Quixote goes through the formalities and words of a Latin mass. And, although there is no Host, bread, or wine, he gives Sancho Holy Communion in mime.

Then he seems to become aware of him.

"*Compañero.*" It is an untranslatable Spanish word expressing deep affection. The two have grown to love and respect each other.

Slowly Quixote slips to his knees and into Sancho's arms. He dies a contented man.

"Is it more difficult to turn empty air into wine, than wine into blood?" says the benign Superior to Sancho.

In the eyes of his late friend, Sancho had taken Communion.

All the way through our recce, I talked to Leopoldo about his time with Greene and how scenes in the book came about, and I saw the film more and more vividly in my mind as I learned about the two central characters. The truth is I couldn't resist it, and soon it was pencil to paper to get down the beginnings of a new screenplay.

Meanwhile, it was also on to business and estimating a budget. A gentleman, in his late middle age, Franco someone-or-other, was brought in by our "film contact" in Madrid to advise me on prices—local working practices and the like. For doing the sums I used the calculator I still use today (and I've only replaced the battery twice since), but it refused to cooperate when adding up pesetas—just too many zeros at the end. Thank God they now have euros.

In terms of cost, we could handle plenty of zeros in Spanish currency on paper, but, when converted into sterling, the final figure was also too high. For a moment it looked as if Muir Sutherland was not going to get his Spanish movie. But, no, it couldn't be lost.

"Muir," I said over the telephone to him. "There has to be someone out here who can look at the production laterally—fresh, young thinking, someone who can take a crew on the road."

"No need to go on the road. Stick in one place—Spain looks like Spain everywhere."

"No it doesn't. La Mancha's nothing like Galicia."

He knew it well enough, but I suppose he was checking out my integrity.

Bottom line, Muir came up with Paco Lara, an experienced filmmaker who worked out of the mainstream. Within two days we had cracked it.

Back in London.

"There's still the other matter of Graham Greene's approval of the script." Rather tentatively I said I was penning it.

"Why not?" smiled Lloyd. "Once you're done fly out to Antibes and get him to sign off on it. Come back to us then."

Johnny Goodman was generous again.

"Take Sally-Ann with you; you'll probably need some feminine comfort!"

By now, after many hours spent traveling, rereading the book, visiting potential locations, and meeting people on whom the characters were based, the screenplay was written in my head—technically it just needed another two weeks to put on paper. All the while I could see no one but Sir Alec Guinness as Quixote.

With the typed-up document in my briefcase, Sally-Ann and I boarded a plane to the south of France. I felt half confident because Leopldo had already read the first twenty pages in Madrid and had telephoned Graham Greene to say, "We have our filmmaker." (It turns out that he was more avid to see the movie made than almost anyone else.)

A Saturday in summer 1984—Nice Airport with Antibes only a few kilometers to the southwest.

And my confidence began dropping. What was I doing here with my humble adaptation of a book by one of the world's greatest living writers? After all, I had started my professional life as a clapper boy!

We got off to a bad start.

"Your room is not booked until Monday," said the hotel clerk rather pompously.

"Oh!" The arrangements for my visit had been made through Hugh Greene to his brother. "But do you have space?"

"*Mais oui.*"

Nothing to do for two days but relax and mentally bite my fingernails as the confidence thingy continued to ebb away.

Sally-Ann persuaded me to go to the beach with her. Too hot after half an hour—back to the room for a siesta.

The phone rang.

"Neame?"

"Er—yes."

"Greene here. Wanted to check you'd arrived all right. The flights into Nice are generally a shambles."

I explained about the hotel booking.

"Hopeless! They don't seem to listen to what they are told. I made the reservation for today."

At least I wasn't on the "hot seat"—yet.

"You've got the script?" he demanded.

"Yes."

"Better bring it round now."

He gave me directions, and I walked the few blocks to his apartment building.

Was I crazy? No one but Sally-Ann and a typist had read my completed efforts.

His apartment was modest. Small sitting room lined with books, tiny kitchen, and just one bedroom.

He took the screenplay.

"I'll read it immediately. Why don't you come back for a drink at seven o'clock?"

Our relationship had been very formal, and I knew we had to break down some barriers.

"My wife is with me, so I'll tell you what, we'll come along for a drink on the condition that we can take you out to dinner afterwards."

He seemed a bit thrown.

"I think there's a pie in the fridge. We could have that," he volunteered.

"No. We'll take you out to dinner."

"Are you sure? You'll be able to reclaim the cost? You won't be spending your own money?" he asked in genuine concern.

Four hours later with glasses in our hands . . .

"I haven't finished reading yet, but I've some notes I'd like you to consider. The first one is the words "Draft screenplay" written at the front. Remove the "Draft" and simply call it 'Screenplay.'"

We had a wonderful time over dinner with Graham's only disappointment being the absence of his beloved Yvonne.

"She'd have so much enjoyed the evening."

Yvonne Cloetta, who we were to meet before our brief trip ended, was archetypal French chic. In her mid-sixties, she was petite with short silver hair, a warm smile, and the ready, attractive half-tinkling, half-husky laugh of a smoker. So pretty, so fun loving.

Theirs was, in a way, an odd relationship. Yvonne was married, and even though her children were by then grown up, she felt it her responsibility to keep the status quo, and thus she would spend what time she could with Graham while carrying on with her everyday home life. They had originally met in West Africa in 1959 (he was there working on A Burnt-Out Case), and they had simply fallen in love. He went to the south of France to be near her. They were truly a couple and naturally so.

By coincidence the room in the hotel we had been allocated was the one he had been given when first moving to Antibes. And there we spent three or four days going though the script with a fine-tooth comb. Only small changes needed, but Graham's enthusiasm was as high as it could have been. If I explained how something wouldn't work for the production the way he suggested, he dropped the issue. Working alongside this superman of a writer was like no other experience I have had or ever will have.

"Casting?" he asked.

I batted the ball back to him.

"Alec Guinness would be perfect in my view," he said.

Absolutely!

I knew they were old friends, so I said, "Could you write him a personal letter saying how much you want him to play the part. But don't date it—I'll send it when the time is right."

Willingly he complied (I still have a precious copy of the letter in his neat small handwriting).

The right time came when I met with the bosses of Euston and Thames.

"Okay, you've proved the budget, and Greene has approved the script. Now we need a lead actor"

Postage stamp on envelope . . .

Time went by. No reply from Guinness.

One week, two weeks, three weeks . . .

Four weeks, and Graham called from France.

"Alec doesn't feel he is right for the part. I told him I disagreed."

Leopoldo called from Madrid.

"Guinness will be Monsignor Quixote, I am certain."

"Please God!"

"Every day I pray."

Still more time passed with no commitment from the actor.

Then out of the blue word came that he was prepared to take on the role. I have no factual knowledge of why the decision was made, but in my opinion one of the reasons was because Guinness found himself, for some reason, unable to go against Graham's wishes.

I telephoned him at his Sussex home. "I am so delighted," I said, "You are our perfect Quixote."

"I don't think I am at all," he replied primly.

"Oh, yes."

"Please, Christopher, allow me to know myself."

I had known him for many years (he had made five films with my father) and had always been self-deprecating—it was best ignored.

Thames/Euston . . .

"Can I now make the film for you, please?"

As may have been expected, Muir was the most positive. I have to say Lloyd didn't object, and, with a smile on his face, Johnny said, "I'm not the best judge as the last ten pages of the script are in Latin, and I've no idea what they're about."

With apologies to the reader for breaking an earlier promise, I pushed the boat out with, "And it really should be filmed on 35 mm."

"Agreed," from Muir without the hint of an argument. "When will you start filming?"

"Once a director is in place."

"I don't wish to appear overly influential," Alec said in his ever-polite manner, "but I have recently worked with Rodney Bennett and believe he would be a valuable asset."

Obviously I chose to follow through on his lead.

Rodney knew about *Monsignor Quixote* from Alec. Not a month before he had seen him playing Shylock at the Chichester Festival Theatre, and over supper they had discussed the project. He has never admitted it to me, but I suspect Rodney was (altruistically) also influential in getting Alec to agree to the role.

Initially he seemed hesitant about being the director—something inherent in him that I came to know and respect. He is the sort of person who fully engages brain before speaking.

"The danger with the subject is it can become too picaresque," he said.

I gave him the script so he may judge for himself.

And waited . . .

Eight days later I called his home only to learn he was away for a week.

Six days more, and he phoned me back and seemed somewhat surprised that we were seriously offering him the job.

"Yes," he replied in answer to my repeated formal offer. "I'd love to direct—if you're really sure you want me."

Thank God! What a great tower of strength he turned out to be, and for the better part of twenty years he has remained one of my closest and most loyal friends.

The final piece of the package was the casting of Sancho.

"Leo McKern would be excellent," Lloyd stated over an evening drink in the office (he got into the way of dropping by at about six and it was always a well-spent hour together).

McKern had starred in Thames' series *Rumpole of the Bailey*. He had a very lived-in face and a glass eye, which made him all the more interesting to look at.

"Mind you he'll probably turn it down," Lloyd continued. "He turns most things down. But I'll drop him a line and ask him to call you."

He didn't turn it down—loved the script and was eager to work with Alec.

The time had come to do a full recce in Spain. Rodney and me with Paco Lara (our Spanish production manager) and Leopoldo coming along too (chattering and laughing all the while). Plus some old colleagues—Malcolm Burgess as associate producer-cum-accountant, Clifton, art director Roy Stannard, and cinematographer Norman Langley (the first time we had been together since *Danger UXB*).

The latter showed a certain lack of enthusiasm, and on the third evening I asked him why.

"I'm perfectly happy, but none of the locations we've seen so far present me with any great challenge," he informed me.

"You wait—we've got one up our sleeves for you."

Two days later we entered the church at *Valle de Los Caidos*.

"Bloody Hell!"

It is a massive underground chamber—probably a hundred yards or more long and lit by low lanterns at either side.

"How am I supposed to light this?" he complained.

"Sure you'll work it out Norman."

Spain is full of *paradors*, hotels at affordable prices, many of them being old monasteries or the like. The one we stopped at in Carballiño the following night was particularly lovely, and the most delicious olives were served as accompaniment to drinks. That's when Clifton had his brush with nonvegetarianism. He couldn't resist the olives and had four in a row.

"They really are great—never tasted anything like them."

"That's because they're stuffed with anchovies," Malcolm remarked dryly.

Poor Clif turned ashen—and, probably unfairly, the rest of the gang burst into laughter.

Within a week all the locations across the country had been found and secured, bar one—*Valle de Los Caidos*.

"*Non!*"

Franco's still extant and still powerful supporters looked on it as a temple where they could openly mourn their revered generalissimo. Besides no cameras were allowed inside, we were reminded.

Paco Lara, something of a rebel when it comes to unilateral rules (thank God), was irate.

"Spain is a democracy now, and public property is the property of every Spaniard." He was sounding a little like Sancho.

He decided to take the matter to higher levels—eventually to government levels.

A producer's (oh, and yes, a screenwriter's) dreams were coming true with the casting in London—Ian Richardson (as the Roman Bishop), Rosalie Crutchley, Maurice Denham, and other top-notch thespians were quickly signed up. With a Graham Greene story and Sir Alec Guinness and Leo McKern "attached," why would they not come along? Particularly as there was the added bonus of having a few weeks of spring in Spain. Sir John Gielgud's agent even called asking if his client might play Quixote's own domineering bishop. After much thought, Rodney and I decided not to go down that route. Why ever not? The bishop is talked about a lot up front and remains somewhat of a mystery until his one scene with Quixote. By according Sir John an up-front screen credit, which assuredly we would have to have done, we would have given the character away to the audience. Instead Graham Crowden was cast and gave a superb performance.

Our start of principal photography in April 1985 was racing up on us and still no breakthrough on *Valle de Los Caidos*.

Paco had approached Pilar Miró, a well-respected director with strong Socialist leanings who, at the time, was head of the government-run Film Commission. She caused quite a stink in Parliament because she passionately felt all filmmakers must have freedom of speech and no barriers should be put in their way. One of her own films openly attacked the practices of the Guardia Civil, and consequently those in their "ivory towers" were a touch afraid of what she might do next.

I flew to Madrid for the day to check out a location where we could film the riot scene. It had been decided not to do this in Galicia, as it might cause some sort of public outcry from the strong supporters of "putting the Virgin up for sale." (To play it absolutely safe, Roy was going to build the front of a church in a small courtyard, thereby keeping us well out of the reach of any offended church officials.)

That evening I was waiting to board the flight back to London when I overheard two silver-haired men in smart black suits. They were talking earnestly, but, not understanding Spanish sufficiently, I had no idea about what—and I didn't care anyway. Suddenly I heard the name "Alec Guinness" mentioned two or three times.

Instinctively I knew their conversation concerned our filming at Franco's "Sacred Shrine," and it just might have been that a decision had been made.

This was confirmed the following morning, when Paco telephoned to say we had been granted permission. Tenacity!

While nearly all the cast and crew flew to Madrid for the commencement of filming, Leo went by train—a journey time of around twenty-four hours. He was terrified of flying. He had been airborne many, many times, and then suddenly he was seized by a panic attack as an aircraft started its roll down the runway for takeoff. Releasing his seat belt, he had raced up the aisle and demanded of an astonished steward two bottles of gin. "Now!" Realizing what was happening, the man had instantly complied. Leo vowed never to fly again. (On completion of *Quixote*, he planned to sell up in England and, with his wife Jane, return to his native Australia. And his treasured car would go too. It was a very, very long sea passage, and he had only just set foot on terra firma in Sydney when he got a phone call. Thames wanted him back to do more episodes of the *Rumpole* series. He had no choice but to return by air and, hey-presto, his phobia was cured.)

The one and only moment of fractiousness throughout the schedule came from Leo. After Quixote's crash in the car, three monks and Sancho carry him on a stretcher toward the bedroom. Down a long, stone-flagged cloister—from beginning to end. Leo lost his grip on his handle, and Alec was unceremoniously tipped onto the floor. Leo was extremely cross with himself!

Filming around El Toboso. Wonderful patches of sun and shade dappling the red countryside and making the windmills burn white at one moment and turning them into silhouettes the next.

Rodney Bennett and I drove back together to our hotel in a nearby town. As we approached the "Plaza Mayor," I spotted Alec sitting by a fountain, reading a book.

"What in God's name is he doing there?" I said.

"Haven't the foggiest."

Getting closer, we discovered it was not Alec but a native of La Mancha.

Nearing the hotel, another oldish countryman stepped out in front of the car and nearly got himself run down.

"Idiot!"

Not a native, it was Leo, who turned and waved his apologies.

It was quite extraordinary how our two leading players had immersed themselves into the roles and become part of everyday life.

Another example of this was during the first of several visits to the location by Graham along with Leopoldo.

Lunch was being taken in some hall or other when Alec entered (in costume). Leopoldo rose to his feet.

"Where are you going?" I asked.

"It is a matter of courtesy to pay one's respects to the parish priest."

One of the most fascinating things I have ever witnessed was the growing affinity between the two actors. It followed exactly the same line as the Quixote/Sancho relationship. They hadn't met before the film, but before the end, they had become the firmest of friends—more often than not having an evening drink and dining together.

There was a wonderful moment when we were staying in a magnificent hotel in León (oddly still half a working monastery). The two were in the bar, chatting away to one another when a busload of American tourists came in. Within moments they had spotted Leo.

"Oh, my! It's Rumpold" (they always end with a "D"). You are Rumpold, aren't you?"

Leo, like Alec, was a shy man. But . . .

"Yes," he admitted.

They talked to him for a while longer, and he responded politely. Then they turned to Alec.

"And who are you?" asked the foremost lady.

"He's my agent," said Leo quickly, and Alec gave her one of his crescent moon smiles.

The attention of the party returned to Leo.

Alec was an utter joy to work with, always thoughtful to others and his performance beautifully prepared—a man with great humility. If there was a fault with him, it was the latter. He was perhaps overly humble.

Occasionally another side of him would emerge. Coming past a table where some of us were having dinner, he heard us talking about a zoo. He then told us of a visit he had made to the zoo in Berlin and the little boy who was watching the bears while chattering away animatedly to his mother. Alec went on to give us a private performance of all three characters—he obviously relished the part of the bear most, and within moments we were holding our sides from laughter as he impersonated its short walks back and forth.

"Rodney," he said to our director as he was preparing to shoot a scene outside León Cathedral. "I hope you don't mind my suggesting it, but I've had a thought. The first part of the scene is really Leo's, and therefore you might keep the camera on him and shoot me from behind."

Not ten minutes had passed before Leo approached Rodney and suggested the same in reverse. (Later, when editing the film, one of the hardest things to handle during Quixote and Sancho's duologues was cutting away from either of the actors. Both "held" the screen even when simply listening to the other—one was aware of their inner thoughts. We had to be tough on ourselves over that.)

The high regard we all had for the gentle Rodney was virtually tangible. Yes, he was focused on the film, yet he always found time for everyone. Perhaps a short exchange or a longer chat if time permitted. He even held a cup of tea for an electrician who was called away to make some minor adjustment. It was evident that the cast and crew, English and Spanish alike, would eat out of his hand—he could have got them to do anything. This was nicely borne out when he had completed a take involving only Leo looking at Quixote's empty car after the priest has been kidnapped by the bishop's men.

"I'd like to go again with you giving a slightly longer look offscreen to the car."

"Why?" asked Leo. "It seemed right to me as it was."

"We can afford a bit more time for your realization of what must have happened."

"I don't agree."

Rodney didn't argue the point and showed not a degree of being put out when he pointed and said to the camera crew, "Okay, the next shot is over there."

"No wait," said Leo. "If you want another take, let's do it."

"Honestly it's not important."

"Yes it is," responded Leo.

"No, we can leave it."

"Rodney, I'd like to do another take."

And so it was. Clever, clever Rodney.

Thanks to the careful planning of Malcolm, Clifton, Liz Bunton (now a production coordinator), and others, the filming went by without incident. In fact it was a stress-free experience for all, and we certainly succeeded in what we had set out to do. Measured in a straight line, the unit covered 1,400 kilometers—sometimes filming in a town or the countryside for half a day and then moving on—*Monsignor Quixote* was undeniably a "road movie."

The final day of photography was at the infamous *Valle de Los Caidos*.

Cameraman Norman Langley had overcome the difficulties of lighting such a vast cavern by using the fastest film emulsion speed currently available. He would then give instructions to the laboratories to "force" develop the footage, a process whereby technically underexposed images could be brought out more.

During the lead-up, I had constantly nagged Paco to get us written permission to be there, but try as he might, no bureaucrat was prepared to attach his moniker to a piece of paper that might have got him into trouble with those of Franco's cronies whose voices were still heard.

Spain had not yet become part of the Common Market, and, a democracy or no, it maintained its own, sometimes draconian, rules.

On arrival at the location, the crew were reluctantly admitted by the wearers of grim faces—"Never seen such a thing!" they seemed to express. And as for having a large generator parked beneath the steps of the arced Fascist entrance chamber—"Well really! It's too much!"

But no one was outwardly hostile—Pilar Miró's daunting (unseen) presence must have been equal to the generalissimo's memory.

Something still niggled—something that can happen unexpectedly anywhere—our last batch of rushes could get mislaid (or even impounded at the airport by two silver-haired men in smart black suits), and damage might occur in the camera. We played it safe and after each shot mounted a second camera and film magazine on the dolly or tripod and reshot it. As a result we had two sets of the material. It proved worthwhile.

I personally carried the second set of rushes back to England as hand baggage and on arrival in London went straight to the Rank Laboratories to view the set sent in the evening before.

Problem: One shot, the most important shot of all, showing the vulgarity of the place in full, had a flare on it—an aberration of light on the lens caused by one of the actual lanterns on the church's walls. Normally such a thing can be seen by the camera operator at the time of filming, but under those circumstances of exceptionally low light it was utterly impossible for Geoff Glover to pick up. We had to keep our fingers crossed for the second set, which would go through the "bath" that night.

Early in the morning to the labs—running the footage at high speed until we reached the all-important shot—Quixote and Sancho walking toward the distant tomb of Franco. Then at exactly the same instant there was the flash of the lantern flare. But it was short—maybe only a second—and unquestionably could be dealt with by "plastic surgery." Phew! Just the slightest movement of position as the second camera had been secured to a tripod or by our actors taking a slightly different path had saved the day.

A first-rate musical score was written by a Spaniard—introduced to us by Muir—which captured the spirit of the country without being sentimental (which pleased Rodney). So smitten was I with it that I asked Thames, who planned to release a long-playing record of the music (performed by the English Chamber Orchestra) if I might write some blurb for the cover. Part of it reads,

> It was essential to find a composer for this film who knew all the elements and backgrounds that were part of our story. Antón Garcia Abril was that composer. After our first meeting we knew his thoughts and ours about the subject were in harmony, even though he spoke little English and we little Spanish. The music was to be integral to the film and at the same time had to echo the feelings within the characters.
>
> Towards the end of the film, a monk at the Monastery of Osera, which is cradled in the Cantabrian Mountains, explains to an American visitor "All Spaniards are romantic, so sometimes we take windmills for giants." In this music, Garcia Abril has expressed the timelessness, the colours, the awe and romance of Spain.

The only disappointment came when Thames Television suddenly decided, in their wisdom, to bring forward the scheduled airdate in 1986 to late 1985. So there was not enough time to publicize the film properly. Despite this it was greatly enjoyed by the audience with high viewing figures, and because of its slightly longer running length to the norm for its slot, *The News at Ten* was shunted back by ten minutes.

Some reviewers carped a bit: This is a British trait—if a film, series, or play is "different," it needs "putting in its place"! This was not the case overseas, where it received nothing but praise.

From the *New York Times* came, "This little film, intelligent and compassionate, is very special."

Unquestionably it remains very, very special to me.

The members of the British Film and Television Academy nominated *Monsignor Quixote* as Best Single Drama and Alec as Best Actor (on television). What I fail to understand is why the film was only ever played once in the United Kingdom—and never ever in Spain! But it is far from all over.

There was a screening at the British Film Institute in late 2002 as part of a season to commemorate the work of Alec Guinness, and, to my surprise and pleasure, it held up beautifully. And in October 2003 it was run again, this time at the Graham Greene Festival. There is no question the 150 members of the audience "went along" with the picture all the way. Both Rodney and I gave a talk afterward and vastly enjoyed the pursuant question-and-answer session.

Someday someone will discover this little gem in a vault and present it to a much wider audience.

What a magnificent stroke of luck for me—I had the once-in-a-lifetime privilege of working with the crème de la crème.

Postscript

Odd request over the telephone in early 1987 from George Roman, artistic director of the highly reputable Northcott Theatre in Exeter.

"I would like to present this story on stage," he said in a thinly disguised Hungarian accent.

"On stage? It's centered around a car journey!"

"Yes, I know."

"Impossible in the theater."

"I think I can find a way—trust me."

I did, and he succeeded.

Graham flew over from France especially to see a performance and expressed his approval. Somehow Rocinante appeared to traverse the 1,400 kilometers convincingly.

This foray of mine into the theater was not to be the last—and not my last with George. Well, with the halcyon years of television drama about to become dulled as a result of noncreative commercialism, what was a chap going to do in the new millennium?

Leave it be for the moment.

Graham's warmth and friendship was enduring, and whenever he was in England (more frequently than we were in France), he, Yvonne, Sally-Ann, and I would meet. Sally-Ann had found the way to his heart—English sausages and mash. Very informal evenings.

"Ahh 'Gr'hmm'" (Yvonne's French pronunciation of his name), "Why don't you do as Christopher says and take off your jacket and tie?"

Her light scolding, mixed with a smile, so well expressed her love for him, and his compliance was an exact reflection.

When Graham died in 1990, it felt like the loss of a trusted uncle.

At a reception following a memorial service in London, Yvonne mentioned how a week before his death he had been going through some diaries and came across an entry concerning one of his trips to visit us in Spain. He said he thought *Monsignor Quixote* was his favorite film based on his work.

Ephemera . . .

Alec Guinness told me that when he was on stage in New York, a middle-aged couple had gone up to the box office and asked if this was the play starring "Alec Gwines." The woman behind the glass corrected them, "Alec Guinness."

"Gwines," they countered.

"Well he pronounces it Guinness."

"Then tell him he's wrong."

Suggestion for dinner . . .

Paella—rice with saffron and any kind of meat and any kind of fish, cooked how you like, but add a copious amount of wine.

To accompany the dish, a chilled rosé, preferably from the Rioja region.

Ice cream (bit of chocolate).

Thick, black coffee. Very, very thick. With an iced "Sol y sombre" (fifty-fifty cognac and sweet anisette).

As a whole the above are the basic ingredients of the kind of meal Monsignor Quixote and Sancho would have enjoyed along the way. And so did all of us!

~

CHAPTER SIX

Nobody Ordered Blizzards!

Ronald Neame has had a most rewarding career as a filmmaker—cinematographer on movies like *In Which We Serve*, the producer of the definitive Charles Dickens adaptation *Great Expectations*, and the director of classics such as *The Horse's Mouth*, *Tunes of Glory*, *The Prime of Miss Jean Brodie*, and the blockbuster *The Poseidon Adventure*.

We had often talked over the idea of working together, but until 1985, there seemed to be no suitable subject. Well, there had been one *Foreign Body* based on a novel by the journalist Roderick Mann—a rags-to-riches comedy about an Indian immigrant to London—but it was impossible to mount because there was no Indian star known to an American and European audience. This suddenly changed when Victor Banerjee appeared as Doctor Aziz in David Lean's *A Passage to India*. Once he had agreed to do the film, Orion Pictures, a somewhat quirky and certainly very astute company born out of United Artists, guaranteed the finance. It was a tight budget, although benefits were made from the conversion of strong U.S. dollars to sterling.

Its production has little relevance to these pages, except to say I was away from television drama and back to the big screen for nine months on a film made for little more than the cost of *Monsignor Quixote*. How could a director so accustomed to much bigger budgets have done it? Answer: Ronnie knew film inside out and was willing to accept certain constraints.

It was another wonderful experience for me personally to work with my father. Just as well, as what was to follow was a bit of a struggle.

Sally-Ann and I had found Spain very alluring. Many have a misconception about the country—they compare it with Tijuana in Mexico or the fly-ridden zones of central South America or even to a Third World nation. Completely false. Spain is sophisticated, immaculately clean (people even sweep the sidewalks outside their houses). The Spaniards are a fun-loving bunch, although their penchant for brass bands gets to be a little wearisome at two o'clock in the morning.

Anyway, we took on a house in a small town called Cadaqués, which lies on the eastern side of the Pyrenees and just where the mountain range drops into the Mediterranean. (Salvador Dalí lived most of his life there, the beaches frequently used for the setting of his paintings and the hollowed-out rocks as models for his sculptures.) In November we were enjoying a justifiable holiday, largely justifiable for my want of a project.

Word came that a Euston miniseries-cum-theatrical film was in trouble. Was I prepared to come back to London immediately? Yes, subject to the script being a good one. It arrived by courier (via Barcelona) the same evening. By midnight all three parts had been read. It was good, but why was it being produced in two versions? The answer was to come two days later when I was in Johnny Goodman's office for a meeting. Also present was John Hambley, who had taken over Lloyd Shirley's job.

It had nothing to do with Lloyd, but an unfortunate situation had happened at Thames during my absence. The BBC had been playing *Dallas* for a number of years but had declined to continue with a new series because the price being asked by the U.S. producers was considered too high. Bryan Cowgill at Thames stepped in and agreed to pay up, thereby acquiring the show for ITV—the commercial independent television network. All hell broke loose. What would have seemed to be a perfectly fair situation was deemed by Cowgill's peers—and the BBC—not to be "cricket." Ridiculous! The outcome was that this highly intelligent man was forced out of the company. Shortly, at his volition, Muir Sutherland was to go his own way too.

John Hambley had proved himself a good television executive and had been part of the team instrumental in securing Thames's ongoing government franchise as a broadcaster. And, as part of a reshuffle of responsibilities, the company's new managing director had decided to put him in charge of Euston Films' affairs.

Bellman and True had originally been developed by Verity during her tenure but had never gone into production. John considered the time was now right. An approach was made to Michael Wearing, a producer from the BBC who had been behind some of the corporation's best work—*Edge of Darkness, Boys from the Blackstuff*.

In turn, Wearing brought in director Richard Loncraine—*The Missionary* with Michael Palin, *Brimstone and Treacle*, and a host of very upmarket TV commercials to his name. As a lucrative sideline he had a company that produced executive toys and gadgets, his maxim being along the lines, "He who gets to Heaven with the most toys has won the game of life."

The two of them could not be more different. Michael, an introvert with hair prematurely gray, was inclined to mumble and pace the carpet as he thought, while Richard—earring, long black hair (giving way to the odd fleck of silver), and a ready smile—has a flamboyant personality and energy. The latter inclines him to walk at a goodly pace, which leaves the likes of me ignominiously running one step in ten to keep up.

Forming a strong partnership, they set to work with the novelist on whose work the script was to be based—an ingenious bank heist involving computers (newish territory in 1986). Bernard Hill played Hiller, a programmer recently out of a job at a company with an arm specializing in bank security. He is recently divorced and has custody of his young son. The two are kidnapped by the robbers, only to be released when Hiller has "cracked" the codes (not encrypted by him), thereby allowing them entry to the vaults. The "contract" is subsequently one-sidedly extended when it becomes obvious he will be needed on the night of "the job." That's an oversimplification of the story, as there is plenty of emotional conflict along the way and, of course, the love interest.

It was to be a three-hour miniseries, and, as always seems to be the case, the budget came in far too high. With due effort it was eventually reduced to a nearly workable amount—but, well, the old story, still too much.

Loncraine came up with a nifty idea. Make two versions, one running 150 minutes (the TV series) and a one-off film of 120 minutes (for theatrical release) with a few linking scenes to aid the abridging. In the past he had worked successfully with George Harrison's company, Handmade

Films, and so approached its managing director with a "pitch." The end result was deficit funding in return for which Euston would allow Handmade to release the one-off in theaters prior to the series broadcast—really quite a smart plan, as cinema films are invariably good publicity for subsequent television exhibition (albeit they are often loss leaders). From Handmade's point of view it would acquire a movie at a fraction of the normal cost. In hindsight I wonder if the "deal" was as good as it appears on paper.

Shooting commenced in November 1986, and before long the wheels started to come off the tracks—probably as a result of insufficient preparation, although I cannot swear to it. Within three weeks the wheels were coming off the axles, and the production was bumping behind schedule—therefore going over budget. Hence my arrival on the scene.

On the surface, stepping into a troubled production can have a degree of appeal—you cannot put a foot wrong! Beneath the surface, though, one easily becomes the villain of the piece as far as the director, cast, and crew are concerned, and that's not helpful to anyone.

Clearly a fine path had to be trod.

The position of the Euston management was that Loncraine was a director in need of firm control and Wearing had not the strength for it. Johnny Goodman holds the same view today as he did then. My regard for Johnny has always been high; nevertheless, we must "agree to differ" over his perfectly understandable assessment of the situation during the early stages of development.

On the day I was to join the team as another producer, I met with Michael over a lunch and began to find out something of his background. I hasten to add, this was not an examination of any sort, but partly to help me tread the path softly and partly to discover his strengths and weaknesses—something we all have if we are human. He had come from the theater—a director—and had subsequently found himself working as a producer for television within the BBC. Probably another oversimplification, but (as recorded above) what I had learned from John Hawkesworth, based on his BBC experiences, is that a producer is more of an executive director. The nuts and bolts of everyday production were left in the hands of managers, who were proficient in the corporation's mechanics. However, Euston had no permanent, full-blown organization behind it, and consequently its producers were obliged to be all-rounders. So Michael had found himself in a world using a very different set of ground rules to his norm.

In the afternoon we headed off to see the unit.

Pretty nerve-wracking . . .

The new boy on the block . . . the hatchet man.

Word had spread—a Euston heavy was coming in. "Watch yourself, mate!"

The only thing I wanted was to see a good project completed and onto the screen—not an entirely altruistic motive, as I needed to keep the rent payments going.

On location—a very large (and at the time disused) building in London's Mayfair.

While Michael went to check on shooting progress, I sort of hovered. The right time to be seen would come.

A woman approached me.

"Hello!" she said in a cheery voice. "Lovely to see you. What are you doing here?"

She was the unit nurse who had worked on *Foreign Body*.

"I just dropped by."

"Super. Come and meet some of the crew."

"I will, in a moment."

"How's Ronnie?" she asked of my father. And thankfully I was able to engage her in a conversation that had nothing to do with the troubles of this production.

Michael reappeared.

"They're a bit behind, so they'll be going on until nine tonight."

As far as I could gather this was par for the course.

Once the crew completed the shot they were working on, we went to the set together.

Met Richard (actually I had met him a few years before in Cannes)— and also Bernard Hill as well as the unit in general. Everyone very polite, although I could feel the tenseness.

Richard, who always wore a very practical blue boiler suit, agreed to a meeting with me at the end of the long day.

He remained courteous even though he thought what was happening was unfair on Michael and unsettling for him and the crew. I concurred and assured him I had no intention of usurping Michael and would give the production my full support. He looked me directly in the eyes, held the look for a moment, then said something like, "I don't trust producers. Not until they've proved themselves."

"Why not give me the benefit of the doubt?"

"Why should I?"

"Because," I still held his look, "I guarantee I will never lie to you or try to pull the wool over your eyes."

"How will I know?"

"Until I've proved myself, you mean?"

"Yes."

"That's why I'd like the benefit of the doubt."

He sat back.

"Richard, I'm here to help with the film, not hinder. The only thing I ask of you is that you talk to me openly and together we'll be all right."

He agreed.

I then moved straight on to the importance of maintaining the schedule from hereon in.

"It'll be a few days before we can fully estimate the cost overage as a result of the slipping, but one thing I can say now is if we get more behind, Euston will move in with very heavy hands."

It would be utterly wrong for me to lay the blame at his door, even for a moment—many, many things can cause delays, and if not kept in check they quickly become cumulative. It was my job to anticipate problems and to try and sweep them away before him. His was to keep right up behind me.

Again he accepted. We had got off to a good start. And only once were we to have a serious standoff. But the truth of the matter was/is that Richard cares only about the good of the project he is making.

By the next day the dust had settled, and Richard willingly talked me through his shooting plans and how he intended to maintain the schedule. He volunteered the same information every day; however, as our trust in one another grew, it became unnecessary.

Hopefully the leak had been caulked. This turned out to be the case—well, almost, as unforeseen trouble lay ahead.

Michael was good to work alongside, especially now that he was able to focus on what he did best—consulting with Richard over creative matters. Although they were both to involve me in this area all the way through, I tended to take a low-key position, viewing myself as more of a godfather than an entirely hands-on producer—too many cooks etcetera.

The task now was to figure out the financial damage.

Phone call to Malcolm Burgess—I knew he was just clear of another project.

"Will you come in on *Bellman and True* with me?"

Malcolm is another of those people (like Rodney Bennett) who needs to think things through after he has been given all the facts. No leaping before looking. This time he had twenty-four hours to decide.

The next day he was with us, and together we started viewing the overall picture.

From a rough guess (guess, because they didn't have accurate figures to work from), Euston had estimated the overage—it was modest enough. But, in actuality, seriously off the mark.

"How much?" "Can't be!" "No, no you must have something wrong," was leveled at me when I went to the head office to give a report of our preliminary findings.

Oddly I felt guilty—as if I shouldn't have allowed such a situation to come about. Really silly. I had been relaxing in Spain when it had.

The summary I gave was the best possible under the circumstances.

"It's caused by the knock-on effect from the schedule. And, I'm afraid, because the production was underprepared in the first place."

I left a small group of not-very-happy people with one last line: "With any luck, we're getting under control, and, as you well know, the footage is very good."

If only that had been the end of the matter.

Two days later I was back with them.

"A number of outstanding invoices have come to light which have not been accounted for."

Heavy sighs.

"Amounting to how much?"

They weren't going to like what they heard.

"Thirty percent over what I told you before."

There was a stunned silence. No alternative but to leave them with it and go back to the location and get on with the production I was now responsible for.

Intentionally I have avoided mentioning actual amounts of money here, and for two reasons. By today's standards the overage would seem to be "reasonable" although still unacceptable, whereas then it was a serious amount of money—also it would be improper for me to quote figures.

The whole situation was oddly reminiscent of the bomb detonated by the Royal Engineers on *UXB*—the earth rippling like rapid waves on the sea. But like those waves, the storm subsided more quickly than it had taken to amass.

Camber Sands, not far from Folkestone in the southeast of England, was a lovely spot and so like the sandy beaches of Spain's Cape Trafalgar, but unfortunately a monstrous nuclear power plant dominates it now. Unsightly as it may be, it formed a backdrop to the garden of the house owned by the late director Derek Jarman. It also made an excellent backdrop for the penultimate sequence in *Bellman and True*.

Hiller, separated from his son, is being held by the successful bank robbers in the darkened back room of a smallish timber house on the beach. A private aircraft will shortly be landing nearby to whisk them all away. He has to find a way of escape so as to be reunited with his son.

By wiring up a large gas canister and connecting it to the light switch, he creates a makeshift bomb. Enticing the baddies into the room, he breaks out in the nick of time before they turn on the light.

The owners of the house we were using had agreed to move into a caravan while filming took place—how sensible of them, even though the explosion would be controlled and the construction crew had erected a false back to safeguard their home against any lasting damage. At least the plans were sound in theory.

On "Action," Bernard Hill (not a stuntman) would get out of the building and run hell-for-leather toward the camera, only just getting clear as the whole thing goes up.

"How is our 'extension' held together?" I asked the construction department.

They must have thought it a very silly question.

"Nails."

"We can't have nails," I said.

"Why can't we?"

"When it explodes they're going to be flying through the air at high speed. One or more could hit our leading man."

Someone went around with a metal detector, and they were all removed. The end result was a freestanding structure apart from a bit of glue and string here and there.

Personally, I have an absolute hatred of filming these kinds of scenes—on one film, when I was a camera assistant, a man had been cut in half in just such circumstances. It was actually his own fault, but it happened nonetheless.

The camera was set up. The special effects team placed their charges. Richard did a run-through with Bernard Hill. Final checks, and we were ready to go.

At the exact second—*Crumphhh!*

Flames and flying balsa wood.

Terrific.

And Bernard Hill didn't have a scratch on him.

One quite serious matter, though. The explosion was bigger than needed, and it lifted the real house off its foundations.

Two horrified owners!

There is only one way to deal with a situation like this. Apologize genuinely and contact the insurance companies. To the best of my belief the parties were still in dispute nine months later. How ghastly for those caravan-bound, innocent people.

In the United Kingdom, robbers are known by their "professional" nicknames. For example, you have "The Peterman," who is the safebreaker—as he holds the keys, he is likened to Saint Peter. You have "The Bellman," whose responsibility is to deal with alarms. And you have "The Wheelman." He is the driver of the getaway car.

The Wheelman in our film was played by one of the best stunt drivers in the industry. But sometimes things can go wrong for everyone.

After the bank robbery, the gang speeds off in a Jaguar. One of the shots was of it taking an "S-bend" at full tilt, and it had to be done late at night to avoid antagonizing other motorists. A sudden fog moved in, and there was, in January, a danger that icing might soon follow. Take one—a filmed rehearsal—and the car held perfectly. Minor adjustments to the camera position. Then take two—the car didn't hold, and it slipped, in sort of slow motion, into some railings. Fortunately no harm came to those in the vehicle, and there was little wrong with the car that a bit of panel beating wouldn't put right. Thank God.

Madness, I thought. Filming cars at high speed in the middle of winter—I had been there before, worn the "T-shirt" and all—but it was the way it had to be.

I should have been prepared for Richard Loncraine's telephone call two days later at around five in the morning.

"Hope you agree. We ought to call the weather cover."

Looking out of the window into the darkness, there was no evidence of seriously adverse conditions.

"Why?"

"It's started snowing here quite heavily."

I didn't argue with him. I was in central London, where the temperature drops less than it does further out of town—and he was further out.

Goddamit! We were only six days off finishing principal photography and holding the schedule we had set weeks before. Now what? Driving to work, I thought there was no obvious way around the disaster but cheered myself in the knowledge that it was inevitable a solution would present itself.

Some smart-ass on the crew said, I felt rather gleefully, "Can't finish on Friday now, can we?"

And that gave me the clue.

"You want to bet?" I replied.

Come what may, we would finish on the designated day and clear up every last shot other than the material involving the high-speed car stuff, which would leave us with three days work to be "picked up" when the weather had well and truly cleared.

"Fine," said Richard. "And you'll keep the key members of the crew on the payroll?"

"No."

"But you'll have to. They may get other jobs and I can't work without them."

I sympathized with him although it was impossible to comply—six or ten people being paid for several weeks.

He was becoming irritable, something I had never seen in him before. "You have to keep Ken on." Ken was the cinematographer.

"I'm sorry Richard, but no."

"We'll see about that!" he said angrily.

Reaching for his mobile phone (a very early one), he walked away. Presumably he was going to telephone Euston Films in an attempt to get me overruled. I don't think he made a call in the end; however, he didn't talk to me for a couple of days and has refused to discuss the matter subsequently. Sensible to put it behind us.

Only twice before had I experienced such weather conditions—winter 1963–64 and winter 1981–82. A bit rum to get them again so soon!

As with *QED*, I called force majeure on the actors who would be needed to complete the car sequence—this would mean they wouldn't be paid during the hiatus. Didn't get away with it the second time around!

While Richard and Michael turned their attention to editing the two versions, the arctic conditions raged on, and it was two months before we were able to get the last few shots in the can.

It turned out to be an absolutely brilliant sequence and was well worth waiting to do properly. (Richard's experience of filming car commercials paid off in trumps.)

Certainly the production had been a toughie—rewarding nonetheless—and at last something absolutely contemporary had come my way. However, I soon found myself yearning once more for the gracefulness of costume drama when a dalliance could spark a revolution—when, somehow, the passion and depth of characters could be deeply explored, largely because of their less speedy lives and times.

With a false start in 1990, it was not until ten years later that I was to rejoin the world in which I felt most comfortable, and it was a project very far removed from commercial television.

Postscript

The theatrical film of *Bellman and True* was critically acclaimed in the United States, but one doubts it showed much of a profit (if any), as it is "art house" material rather than mainstream. A few years later parts of the novel were filmed again in *The Real McCoy* starring Val Kilmer and Kim Basinger. Presumably, up front, this was considered a more commercially viable package, but the result was, reportedly, disappointing.

There is, however, in my judgment, a flaw in our film. The miniseries, which ended up running for three and a half television hours, is able to go into sufficient character development, whereas, perforce, the two-hour film could not compete on the same level. Won't go into it too deeply here.

It's a pity a record was never released of the end title music.

After the explosion at the house, Hiller rescues his son from elsewhere, and the two go to Heathrow and board a flight to Rio de Janeiro—with the money from the heist. For the titles Richard devised a long tracking shot across a cartoon map of their route across the Atlantic ending up with the statue of Christ on Corcovado Peak. Played over this is the famous Scottish song "D'ye ken John Peel at the break of day . . ." and the legendary Lonnie Donnegan sang it. Donnegan had enjoyed huge popularity with his skiffle band in the 1950s and 1960s, regularly hitting number one in the charts. The point of the whole thing is that John Peel was a huntsman, and four of his hounds were called Ranter and Ringwood, Bellman and True.

On the matter of titles, this was the first time I encountered sharing a producer's screen credit with someone I never met—George Harrison. Clearly an indication of what lay ahead whereby hoards of people, always valued for their financial input, demand, in return, screen recognition for a job they have not done and would be ill equipped to do. Producing means producing—not simply funding.

Richard Loncraine was rightly given praise for his work and has continued to enjoy an excellent career. A notable example is his film of Sir Ian McKellen's innovative *Richard III*. Michael Wearing returned to the BBC and for many years headed the Serials Drama Department and was responsible for a formidable body of work.

Johnny Goodman came out of it all with his ever-ready sparkling good nature still intact. Tragically, though, it was the beginning of the end of a terrific phase of his life. But not the end of Johnny by any manner of means.

CHAPTER SEVEN

~

A Rose among the Thorns

I hugged him tightly, this shortish man of barely sixty, and somehow sensed the dampness of tears not actually shed.

Johnny Goodman was clearing his office at Euston Films, and I had brought him a small leaving gift. He had certainly served the company well for the better part of ten years, but with "new brooms," he no longer felt he was in the right place. He had not been forced to quit but considered it wiser to take up an offer to run a similar operation for another Independent Television network company.

Bit of a mistake as it happens. Most of the time he sat in their London office, largely alone, and knew little of what was going on at the company's studio. One of the few tasks he was given was to find a producer to watch over a half-hour movie to be made in Budapest. Kindly he put me forward. Three weeks in a beautiful city (particularly the old Castle District of Buda, where one could wander back into the past and imagine wayward princesses partaking of mugs of steaming hot chocolate—well—with cobblers, if one's to keep the fairy tale alive). Fortunately, with the advent of laptop computers, I was able to keep one eye on a desperately mediocre production (thankfully no screen credit for me!) and the other focused on writing.

The filming experience introduced me for the first time to the production of material based solely on advantageous financial rewards—"deal-led" situations where quality was low on the list of priorities.

My second and, thankfully, last experience of that was to occur six months later—the interim period being taken up with the stage production of *Monsignor Quixote* (as rewarding a time as it was when making the movie).

A "neat" package of six two-hour TV films was offered to me to produce—frankly I cannot bear to mention the generic title for fear I may be found out (IMDB has missed it!). Have to say I was a bit suspicious about the whole thing from the start; however, my agent, whom I held in high esteem, told me she had greater respect for a producer who was in work than for one who was not.

Simply three market "territories" (it could have been Germany, Hong Kong, and South Africa but wasn't) fully funded two productions each and in return got the other four for nothing—cheap at a third of the price. Cardboard characters and mayhem as one producing country vied to outdo the others in the "art" of filmmaking. Please! Creative compromises—bowing to so-and-so's investment requirements—and compliance with tax laws around the globe—the lawyers having a ball with their charges and a lot of my life spent wading though interminable contracts. Paperwork is becoming a world nemesis.

Each episode was to be of two hours, and herein lies a stumbling block, which is hard to overcome. Most series will have a central set—say, the protagonist's home or office—and maybe fifteen minutes per hour could be filmed there quickly and efficiently, thus allowing extra time for scenes elsewhere. However, double that for a two-hour show, and it would mean thirty minutes in the main set, which (most likely) would become thumpingly boring.

Fortunately I had a "break clause" in my contract and chose to exercise it after the first two episodes.

Just as one can have a little warning shiver in September as a precursor to winter, the first real hint of tarnish could now be seen tingeing the gold of television drama—or so it seemed to me. Question—was it only me it was happening to?

For some time the BBC Series Drama Department had been casting an envious eye at the fluidity of productions coming from the growing number of independent organizations such as Euston Films, and they now wanted to be a part of that world. Would I come and do a series there? Yes, how exciting. It was to star a popular actor who was also the writer of several of the scripts—and he was bloody good. Trouble was he wanted to be in entire control of the show as well. It was a feasible idea (just) but would end up making me redundant before I had even started. Right from the outset, it was clear we were going down different paths and I would have to fight every step of the way to bring the merest crumb to the table.

Steady, though, if I wasn't careful, I would find myself resigning from a well-paid job.

"There's a problem," I stated clearly to the corporation's current head of the Series Department. "As the producer, it is incumbent upon me to advise you that you need to replace either the leading actor or the producer." A bit pompous, I accept, but intentionally so. There was no chance of his sacking the actor, without whom there would be no series, and so I was left in the "drop" position with fees to be paid in full!

(Really very stupid of the BBC's business affairs crowd—why hadn't they put me on a step deal in case things didn't work out?)

Not entirely satisfactory because, apart from the money, I wanted to be an active producer.

"How about this?" said the drama chief. "Jean Marsh and Eileen Atkins have come up with an idea which shows some promise. There's not much to go on, three pages or so—do you want to take a look at them?"

You bet I did!

Jean and Eileen, both superb actresses in their "day jobs," had previously collaborated on the creation of *Upstairs, Downstairs* (produced by John Hawkesworth), and what they now proposed was equally as good.

The House of Eliott is set in the 1920s. Two sisters in their early twenties, daughters of a widowed doctor, live a comfortable suburban existence. The father is killed in a riding accident, and, their sorrow aside, they are devastated to learn he was in debt up to his eyeballs. Simply the Eliott sisters must work to exist—work in a world largely closed to gentlewomen. Both have flair and are naturally elegant dressers, so they decide to set up a fashion house. The potential for stories about the glamorous world of haute couture played against the sweatshop environment of seamstresses, of Mayfair society against the slum life of London's East End, was enormous. Added to this Jean and Eileen were a joy to be with.

Almost immediately it started going rotten. The first script was lackluster—formulaic. Plus my lady script editor was pushing hard for the inclusion of a strong strand about female emancipation. It wasn't on—some years before Verity Lambert had made the perfect series about the subject (*Shoulder to Shoulder*), so why tread old ground?

Soon the script editor left and declared to all and sundry, "Christopher Neame is impossible to work with."

While this little disruption was being sorted out, I turned my attention to production matters. It would be great if we could film (or record) the major part of the series at the BBC's Ealing Studios. There the interior of "The House of Eliott" could be built, with its entrance near to the door of the soundstage. And outside we could clad the side wall of the stage opposite to turn it into a London street—cobbles on the ground. Passersby and horses and carriages would add to the effect and provide a genuine backdrop.

"No, you can't do that," the studio manager told me.

"Why not?"

"It'd hinder the day-to-day traffic going around the studio."

What! Was this a place for making films or was it a highway?

Another suggestion. The East End exteriors could be done near to where Sally-Ann and I now lived on the south bank of the Thames in Rotherhithe—plenty of Victorian alleyways to be found.

"No, you can't do that," said the production manager.

"Why not?"

"It'd mean overnights for the crew."

What! Daily I traveled on the Underground to the BBC's offices in West London. All of thirty-five minutes!

The bureaucracy was beginning to get in the way of any original thinking.

"Christopher Neame is impossible to work with," announced the second script editor. At least he added, "Although he is a very nice man."

He resigned.

It came about because I had wanted to do away with what promised to be a boring first episode showing the two Eliott sisters in their comfortable surroundings—seeing the father and taking the story up to his death and funeral. No, no—start after the funeral, with the two principals discovering they are penniless right up front. Instant conflict. And learn about the past along the way.

I hadn't wanted to be overadamant, so I had agreed to let the script editor try and convince me by writing an outline for episode 1 the way he saw it.

Total rubbish!

Meanwhile other good scripts were emerging from highly respected writers, including one from Jeremy Paul (*Danger UXB* and fellow alumnus). At least Jean, Eileen, and I thought they were good, but the drama chief didn't.

Clearly we were not getting anywhere, so it was decided to postpone the show. At least I was paid in full.

About a year later it was restarted with another producer. Jean and Eileen kept me posted and certainly gave me the impression they were unhappy with progress.

I saw only the first two segments, and they were not good. This will come across as churlish, so let me try and put it right. They were both directed by Rodney Bennett (my friend from *Monsignor Quixote*), and he apologized to me (I can't think why) about how poor they were. He had been asked to direct some more episodes, but had politely (Rodney is always polite) declined.

To be strictly honest, the series was well enough received; however, it did not survive very long—it should have been on television screens for five or six years. What a missed opportunity; certainly *The House of Eliott* had started out with the potential of *Upstairs, Downstairs*.

Well, I was out of the BBC, and not too much time passed before all those I had encountered there were too!

I have merely taken time out to write about this experience to prove "You can't win 'em all!"

Back on the upbeat!

Suddenly, from out of the blue, a new Jack Rosenthal script appeared. *Bye, Bye, Baby*—its title coming from the song made famous by Marilyn Monroe. A semiautobiographical work, it tells about Jack or Leo, as the character is called in the film, doing his National Service in the Navy in the 1950s, when conscription was still in existence. With a picture of the Hollywood star stuck on the locker beside his bunk at a shore base in Germany, he "hears" her voice counseling him about how to become a man and how to relate to his contemporaries and his immature girl-friend back in England and how, as a Jewish boy, he might handle the people in whose previously anti-Semitic country he is now barracked.

At an early-on meeting in his North London home, Jack produced volumes of written material. Rather like the stock for a delicious soup, he had continued to boil down the work over a number of years. This is the short answer to why his writing is so pithy—the less simple reason is he is an unsurpassable observer of people: personalities and individual natures. He has the ability to "paint" characters in words that slip effortlessly onto the screen. Sometimes I wonder why he is not sitting on one of the golden (fiberglass) thrones of Hollywood—but it would not suit this down-to-earth man. Jack shares the same kind of humility Graham Greene had and Alec Guinness (in his own particular way). If anyone cared to ask me to name three real superstars, these men are they. Of them all, Jack has the most spontaneous wit, and it does not simply remain on the surface.

The two-hour TV movie was to be backed by Channel Four, if (ho-hum) their budget could be met, and would be produced under the banner of a French company called Paravision. Their British arm was headed by Linda Agran, who, for some years, had worked as Verity's script editor at Euston. My goodness Paravision (United Kingdom) had sumptuous offices in London's Chelsea Harbour with a number of good, although very expensive, restaurants nearby.

One-off films are fun to make because there is an easily definable beginning, middle, and end. Over the course of a series this can become diffused to some extent, and with a miniseries it is tougher still to handle properly—the natural waveform is in danger of slipping over to another episode (having said that *The Perils of Pauline* cliff-hanger endings are always tempting to try and do well).

The amount of funding dictated how Bye, Bye, Baby would be made. And there wasn't a hope of going on location to Germany. In fact, absolutely as much as humanly possible needed to be shot in a studio—just a few daily locations with one interior set that would have been too costly to build. The director designate was Edward Bennett, a man I found to be similar to Richard Loncraine in many ways, primarily that he would fight for the film. Having no choice, he settled for the English version of the German countryside and agreed that the Nene Valley Railway, where we had icily filmed sequences for QED, was a perfect substitute for the real thing. However, he was unhappy about having to film a night sequence on the garish "Reeperbahn"— with its numerous sex "establishments" more prolific than Ireland's pubs—anywhere but in Hamburg. Simply could not be, and another way to create the setting had to be found.

The best studio deal came from Pinewood. As most will agree, Pinewood was, and still is, the number one place to make a movie, and it was a joy to be going back there. My last film on the lot had been twenty years before, but all my life I had known this wonderful studio. Throughout much of my childhood, my father had made films there, and living nearby made it a fantastic second home where the expansive, well-kept grounds were a joy to play in. Once there was even a riding stable, providing horses when required "on set" and offering lessons to children from the neighborhood. I have always loved riding and still do, so it was a special bonus that our offices for Bye, Bye, Baby were located in the now converted stable block. Each day I was to have happy memories of mucking out, getting kicked, and thrown to the ground!

As the sets were being constructed and the budget and schedule finalized by Clifton and Malcolm (who by then had worked with me almost continuously for twelve years), the casting was proceeding in London.

There were, of course, some lovely cameo roles (there always are with Jack), with the running characters being a group of enlisted seamen— not at sea but keeping a watching brief over the airwaves for the movement of any Russian shipping of a potentially aggressive nature—Cold War and all of that. An absolutely top-notch troupe of actors was assembled to support and play off the central character, Leo. The actor for this part was the toughest to find, probably because we had Jack himself as a role model. Funnily enough, the one we finally settled on wasn't Jewish! This was to be a debut film performance by Ben Chaplin, who has since built up an impressive list of credits.

Only one element was not in place. How the hell were we to reproduce the Reeperbahn? The first part of the question was easily enough answered—Pinewood it had to be. There is a massive maze of undercover areas there, connecting stages to workshops, transport bays, and scene docks. Plenty of walls and various passages running between them with iron fire escapes—and the whole remained in semidarkness even on the brightest of days. Reason argued that similar passageways led off the Reeperbahn (and if they didn't, who would take issue with it?).

In the end it was highly effective. The doorway into a grip store was dressed with a brilliantly flashing sign, and the area beyond (representing the main street) had a couple more neon signs, the concrete floor was hosed down, and cinematographer Ivan Strasburg splashed color all around. And thirty extras mingled past the narrow opening.

Our boys rush out of a place of entertainment where they have run into trouble and escape their pursuers by scaling a fire ladder—one of them stark naked. The remainder of the sequence happens on the roof above the Vegas-like "street"—the wider view obscured by another huge electric sign. Yes, it worked very well, but oh, to have had computer imaging then—the backdrop would have been sensational.

Jack Rosenthal is very much a "hands-on" writer and remained on set throughout the filming—he did the same on *The Knowledge*. If I had been the director, I suspect I would have found it disconcerting, but both Bob Brooks on the earlier film and Ed Bennett on this one not only accepted it but also clearly enjoyed his presence. Certainly Jack is someone who adds natural warmth to the surroundings. Some while later I asked him why he didn't take on the director's role himself—he didn't give me a very good answer, just said he would make a lousy director. For someone who is right about almost everything, he's wrong about that in my view—more's the pity.

Bye, Bye, Baby is a thought-provoking film, touching many of those emotions filmmakers are obliged to elicit—and sometimes do.

Postscript

Bye, Bye, Baby won a Prix Europa award in 1992, which Jack collected on our behalf. He also won the Writers' Guild of Great Britain award the following year.

Paravision (U.K.) did not remain active for long—in fact I believe this was the only film they made. Linda Agran and her partner moved to permanent offices at Pinewood and set up their own company.

Conscription (or National Service) ended in Great Britain in the latter 1950s. I was lucky to miss it. No, perhaps not lucky—for many it was a good experience, and young men had an early opportunity to be part of the University of Life. Undeniably they were taught discipline and matured rapidly as a consequence.

CHAPTER EIGHT

~

Kiwifruit and Sauerkraut

Rumor had it that they were an awkward bunch to deal with.

"They" were three of the principal actors in the series *Soldier, Soldier*. Two series had already been made, each of six films, and now another thirteen were to be produced for Central TV.

Johnny Goodman had finally got himself released from the mundane job he had held for around eighteen months and had joined the prematurely white-haired Ted Childs, managing director of Central Films (a similar setup to Euston) as his head of production. In the past Ted had produced at Euston for both Lloyd Shirley and Verity (it all sounds a bit incestuous, but the truth is there were very few of us freelance people working in television at the time, and we all knew one another). Plus he had also been at Consolidated for a short while. By 1992, with many successes to his name, he was considered by the majority to be at the very top of the tree—unquestionably he was the most prolific when it came to commissioning TV product, and inevitably this was a contributory factor leading to the number of successes.

We were just at the point of "delivering" *Bye, Bye, Baby* when Johnny asked me to join the two of them for a breakfast meeting in a London hotel—"Full English," I think the expression is.

There were two projects on the cards. The first was a post–World War II series loosely based on the formation of Cathay Pacific (very loosely, it transpires, because some years later a friend and neighbor in the country, Sir John Swire, gave me a book about the birth of the airline—The Swire Group owns it!). Anyway, it was a good concept with flying and stories of skulduggery, all set in Hong Kong and the South Pacific. Sadly it was not to come to fruition. The other was the continuing *Soldier, Soldier*—this time to be filmed in New Zealand and Germany.

Ted is softly spoken, and his mouth moves little, but I heard him clearly enough when a week or so later he asked if I was willing to head out to New Zealand on a survey prior to producing the show.

A very fair deal was settled between my agent and Johnny, who topped it all off by saying, yet again, there would be a business-class ticket thrown in for Sally-Ann when shooting commenced. This sort of thing is common in Hollywood contracts but not in the United Kingdom. Typically thoughtful of Johnny.

Four days later he and I were to fly out together for a few days in the Southern Hemisphere—Johnny heading onward to Australia and me back to London before going to Germany. Oh, well, get the jet-lag defense kit out of the closet.

The show was devised by Lucy Gannon, a lady who came rather out of left field. Primarily it concerns the lives of regular British soldiers, their wives and families, and their personal struggles and achievements during their U.K. and overseas postings. Technically it was not a "soap," as it was for prime-time television rather than daytime and it had a limited number of segments, but in a way it sort of qualified.

Why do things always happen at the last minute? In order to deliver to the network on time for the scheduled airdate, filming would have to start six weeks hence, but before addressing anything else, I had to try and get my head around the whole idea and so ran the twelve previously produced films several times. It amounted to three days work.

Next it was scripts—only three existed, with just one up to scratch, and another ten stories to be created. All of this with a 25,000-mile round-trip wedged in. Thank the Lord for the associate producer Annie Tricklebank. She would have to, and did, keep her finger on the production pulse (although unfortunately she was not going to be about for the three New Zealand episodes). Another tremendous ally was David Young, the script editor working directly for me.

Up until then my only experience with script editors was at the BBC, and I was unable to hold them in very high esteem—frankly the same applies to those I have encountered ever since, except for David. Initially I confess to having been somewhat chary about him; however, the "ice was broken" by a minor coincidence. We needed to have a meeting before I set off for Auckland, and the best I could offer was for him to be at my home on the morning of departure. I gave him a coffee and told him to make himself comfortable while I packed the last few items needed. When I returned to the sitting room, he asked me an odd question.

"Why have you got several pictures of my ex-girlfriend around the place?"

He pointed to one.

I laughed. "She's my stepdaughter, Kathryn Abel."

He then went on to inform me that he, his wife, and Kathryn and her partner were all still good friends. Somehow or another this gave us a bond.

Only a week had elapsed until we met again in our Soho production offices and were able to spend a little more time together. Both of us had come up with further story ideas, and it was a fruitful day, continuing through lunch at an inexpensive though super Thai restaurant.

"Here's a plan," I said to him on our way out. "What we'll do from now on is come here for a lunch every three days or so and if we unearth the basis of a good plot for an episode we'll charge the meal to the production budget. If we don't the cost'll be down to us personally."

It worked. Although we usually ended up footing the bill ourselves, there were sufficient "awarded" lunches to find enough material for the series.

The following day—Germany.

Münster in Westphalia is a lovely small town that had all but been ripped apart by heavy, Allied air raids during the war—you wouldn't know it today, as it has been meticulously rebuilt brick by brick. For many reasons the event was tragic, made even more so because its inhabitants were known to be anti-Hitler. It is said Münster was home to the Führer's favorite barracks and that a battery of guns was permanently aimed at the

civilians in case they caused trouble. When we went there it was occupied by the Coldstream Guards, who formed part of the Rhine Army.
They were fine hosts to our cast and crew, as were the local townsfolk.

The majority of the ten German episodes could be filmed in or
nearby the barracks, thus making it a very controlled situation, and
Annie had preparations well in hand.

Back to London for casting, signing directors, and pushing on with
the scripts.

The bulk of the actors were in place from the earlier episodes (Holly
Aird, the little girl in *Flame Trees* being one), and only a half dozen or
so new regulars were required. These were selected over a couple of
weeks by Anthony Garner (who was to direct two of the New Zealand
films), the casting director, and myself. Also there were "guest" appear-
ances to be considered.

It was during this period that I met the three actors, who were said
to be awkward, in order to confront them head-on from the start.

"Us?" said the first. "No, we're very good."

Two days later . . .

"We're not awkward," the second answered to my challenge.

And finally . . .

"Never—good as gold we are."

We'll see, I thought and then said to them individually. "All we
want is peace and calm. So if you have any hint of a problem, come to
me personally before trouble occurs."

The only *big* hint of a problem was the bloody scripts. The second
one, written by the clever, young Heidi Thomas, was in good shape
apart from one small matter (or small it seemed at the time), which
could easily be rectified, but the others had to be addressed very seriously. And right *now*! Because Tony Garner was off to Auckland to pick
locations and local actors.

Fortunately Ted Childs, an experienced screenwriter, stepped in to
tackle episode 1, while David Young and I grappled with episode 3. Eventually we sort of got there—and any tinkering could be done on site.

Within a week I flew out to join Tony in what the Maori call "The
Land of the Long White Cloud."

He is a bear of a man with a ready smile for everyone and a calmness in any situation—as would be witnessed (by some) before long. Tony had started his professional life as an actor but shortly switched to behind-the-camera chores. He has directed some good stuff and was lucky to have been given the first series to be made by the BBC in high-definition format. It looked absolutely sensational—3-D almost. A shame the general public could not benefit from the quality in those days (perhaps they should rerun it—believe it if you see it!). What was most important is that *The Ginger Tree* is a well-handled piece of storytelling, and it made me eager to work with its director.

The bulk of our series in N.Z. was to be filmed in a massive military camp near the small town of Waioru right in the center of the North Island. So small was the town, in fact, that it was possible to drive from one end to the other in forty seconds without breaking the speed limit.

It was a tonic to see how the indigenous people merged completely with the Europeans. If there was any friction between the two, it was well disguised. On the first Sunday there, our entire company was invited to a Maori welcoming ceremony, which included rubbing noses with everyone. First the chief (who could have been a lawyer from Mondays to Fridays) gave an address in his native tongue, and then, as the perceived headman of our team, my duty was to reply—mainly in my native tongue. Fortunately, though, I was able to greet them in Maori. True it was like the "Ich bin ein Berliner" bit, but a little longer. Later a couple of our U.K. actors asked me how I had managed it.

"Simple. Did you notice me moving my hands rather a lot?"

"Not really."

"Well, I did. Once I'd been told the words for what I wanted to say, I wrote them down phonetically on the sides of each of my fingers." Talk about the magic of the movies!

It was good to get out of the small apartment Sally-Ann and I were staying in at a nearby hotel. Most days were spent holed up there toiling away on the scripts. Working on a scene to be filmed two days later and faxing pages back to Central in London for their contractual approval. This wasn't easy, as the company's script editors had to have their say (even over the word "nevertheless" versus "however") and David Young needed to spend a lot of time keeping everything on an even keel. Its all very well having wonderful ideas, big or small, but it helps to know the actors who are going to play the scenes, and it helps to know the locations.

Matters got really out of hand on the second episode when the Holly Aird character "Nancy" is about to confront her husband "Paddy Garvey" about a divorce (actually, for personal reasons, she did not wish to remain in the series beyond the three films in New Zealand). The scene called for her to decline Paddy's amorous advances on the grounds she had "The Curse." It was too far-fetched, as couples ready for "action" rarely use such an excuse nowadays—it's only one step up from having a headache. She was in danger of slipping out of character. No, they had to hit the conflict point straightaway—he sensing something was amiss, she finding herself in an awkward position.

My amended scene did not meet with a great round of applause in London, and I was told it had to be filmed entirely as originally scripted because it was funny. Really? The two actors were not amused, nor was Ian Mune. He is an innovative actor-cum-director—a New Zealander by birth (he played "The Reverend" in the magnificent *The Piano*). Currently he was shooting one of the best films in the whole *Soldier, Soldier* series. Gamely the three of them tried playing the scene one evening after shooting—simply it did not work.

Fax to London to tell them so and say "Sorry."

The following morning a fax came back from Central—apparently Ted was absolutely adamant it should be done as it was scripted.

There was not much I could say to that—and to try and talk to him personally on the phone with our watches upside down was nigh on impossible, so we would have to struggle through the scene like troopers in a swamp and wait for the outcome once the material had been viewed in London.

Three days later, another fax. Ballistic. Why had we fucked the scene up?

A little more water had to flow beneath the bridge before the difficulty was resolved.

Sally-Ann was a great support throughout, particularly in relation to the three "awkward" ones.

Except they weren't awkward. Gary Love, Jerome Flynn, and Robson Green were all just as they had said they were in response to my earlier comments. There wasn't an ounce of trouble about them. They were convincing in their performances, had good senses of humor, were never late, and were friendly to everyone throughout the entire twenty-six-week schedule. It was a real pleasure for me shortly to tell them any rumors I had heard beforehand had not been born out and working with them was wonderful.

Each of them looked upon my wife as an ally. As a mother of four children of much their ages, she could talk to them on that level—not over production matters—and never patronizingly. They all became great chums and on days off would take various trips together.

She was particularly excited about a planned white-water rafting adventure. Oh, no, no! It could not be allowed for actor insurance reasons. Unlikely any injury would be sustained, but if it had been (thereby causing loss of filming time) and I had known about it in advance, the underwriters would rightly accuse the company of negligence. It was a pity I found out—hate being a spoilsport. And who else but me was going to tell the boys they couldn't go? They might have become argumentative, but they didn't.

"Look," said the lanky, very laid-back Jerome. "The last thing we want to do is cause any upset and so we'll cancel the trip."

It was as painless as that, and Sally-Ann made up for it by organizing another less risky outing, like going to the top of the extinct volcano Ruapehu—we were pretty confident it wouldn't erupt suddenly. (Mind you, S-A subjected herself to another thrill of which the boys were no part. Imagine a woman in her forties throwing herself over the edge of a canyon on the end of a bungee cord. The video recording of the event is quite funny because as she bounced above the surface of the River Wanganui, her main concern appeared to be that her top was going to come off. Shame it didn't, there would have been an extra turnout for the official rushes if we had run the VHS as an additional entry!)

The third episode, under the guidance of Tony Garner again, started on schedule with only the unresolved "curse" scene hanging in the air from the past.

The general pattern was each story had three strands intercut, and each, in theory, reached its conclusion by the end of the allotted fifty-minute screen time. A strand in Tony's new film concerns an army exercise where our soldiers have to build a bridge over the aforementioned river—good excuse for lines about the "Bridge on the River Wanganui." By the time they got to film this sequence, I would be heading back across the equator for duties in London and Münster.

The last evening in New Zealand was one of the most memorable and warmest occasions in my life. The actors arranged to take over a superb little restaurant (serving the most succulent lamb on Earth), and everyone came along to wish me bon voyage. (Unfortunately Sally-Ann was not present, as we had arranged for her to spend a few days on a Pacific island before returning home—she ended up getting badly sunburned, poor thing.) After the meal was ended our superb cast gave an impromptu entertainment—very funny and very musical plus a lot of witty in-jokes at the expense of the producer! Directly as a result of that terrific occasion, Robson Green and Jerome Flynn teamed up to form a singing partnership for a couple of years—their recordings reaching up high in the charts. Good for them.

At thirty-five thousand feet, I was unaware of what happened in Waioru during my return flight. Most of the shots concerning the building of the bridge were completed, only three or four more to do. The camera was being set up, and Tony Garner was enjoying a well-earned polystyrene cup of tea when he suddenly noticed the bridge was moving "like it oughtn't." Slow motion all the way.

Creak—crack—spurrr-losh . . .

Tony turned to Jerome and said, "Bit rum sometimes, this filming malarkey."

That's an example of the calm way this man can handle a potentially tricky situation. Never mind, Tony got on with something else while the professional soldiers got the bridge reconstructed to a visually acceptable standard within thirty-six hours.

Just two days in London—twelve before filming commenced in Germany.

David Young had e-mailed me two upcoming scripts that still needed some attention and we settled down to the task. (Also made time for a Thai lunch to try and come up with two later stories—awarded.)

Evening meeting with Ted Childs.

I had braced myself for a battle royal over "the curse" scene—willing to put my head on the block if needs must. It had to be reshot properly and shot PDQ.

My case put forward, he simply said, "Didn't work then?"

"No," I answered in a somewhat deflated manner.

We looked over the content together, made a few revisions, and within ten minutes had something we both believed would be okay. Today I still wonder how the entire situation came about in the first place and how half a day of filming (eventually recovered) had been wasted. Was Ted aware of the difficulties? He was a very busy man, and, within the scheme of things, Nancy's period was of minor concern, so I tend to believe he had left it in the hands of others.

As a result of the saga, an idea started forming and, once matured, was to prove a useful defense mechanism.

Directors (seven in all) were dropping nicely into place. Tony Garner was to do more episodes in Germany, and, as a special bonus for me personally, Rodney Bennett came in for two. Ever since *Monsignor Quixote* I had wanted to work with him again. (More recently he had introduced Catherine Zeta-Jones to a wide audience when she played one of the leads in *The Darling Buds of May*.)

By the time shooting commenced in Münster, scripts still remained the biggest worry. We had about four in hand.

Heidi Thomas and Ian Mune's excellent episode gave us a yardstick for future situations. Whereas the personal lives of the characters could always be made to hold an audience's attention, it was the military sections that were in danger of becoming tedious. There's only so much one can do with state-of-the-art military equipment (kindly lent to us unstintingly on the instructions of the Ministry of Defence, who greatly supported the production). As there was no war on, our "soldiers" had to keep up to speed by taking part in large-scale exercises, but those sequences needed conflict like Heidi's script had assuredly supplied. The exercise she devised was one using live ammunition—dangerous! Subtly she let the audience know something terrible was going to happen to one of the characters, which made the scene riveting. Indeed, one young soldier, who the viewers will have got to know and like, becomes overenthusiastic in the excitement of bombardment, runs too far ahead of the field, and is blown to smithereens.

We tried to keep this kind of thing up as much as possible.

The army has one exercise that is a sort of hide-and-seek operation called "Escape and Evasion." Imagining themselves to be behind enemy lines, a group of soldiers must remain in hiding for, say, three days. Meanwhile another group tries to encourage them out and give themselves up. Any trick in the book is allowable. "Jones, a signal from the C.O. Your grandmother's had a stroke and is not expected to live. Report to barracks immediately." Everyone knew the "rules." Mind you, it can (or use to) be a very tough game too—soldiers get caught, blindfolded, interrogated, frightened into believing they face very real physical danger, which could go so far as being handcuffed to an active railway line and left there.

For our story the pregnant wife of one young soldier on this exercise is rushed to the hospital in critical condition. He receives a "signal," but so eager is he to prove himself that he ignores it. The cat-and-mouse situation is very real and offers a lot of suspense. Will she pull through? Will he be got to her in time?

Sometimes Jerome, Robson, and Gary Love would offer up suggestions for their characters.

"Just don't make it easy for me," said Jerome about a scene in which the soon-to-be-divorced Paddy Garvey goes to the home of a German girl he has been dating. It's a foregone conclusion they will end up in bed.

Throughout the short scene, he struggles with himself. Is he being unfaithful? Is he just using the girl? Shouldn't he be allowed a little happiness?

We used a version of Jermome's words to conclude.

"Why do you make it so difficult for yourself, Paddy?" says the compliant girl.

Normally I'm against ad-libbing, as it can sound very phoney, as if an actor is trying too hard. But so good were these boys at it that on several occasions we simply put in the script—*Garvey and Tucker chatter to each other as they walk along the street*—and unfailingly Jerome and Robson would come up with an entertaining exchange. These two are naturally very funny actors and knew their roles inside out.

A pattern was beginning to emerge. As the writing had to be completed quickly, more writers than was desirable were engaged, and it would have been impossible for any of them to have an overview of the series. The task fell to David Young and me. When a script was delivered, the two of us and sometimes the director or Ted would each tackle a strand over the weekend. On the Monday, David stitched the strands together and e-mailed the finished work to Annie in Germany. Then once the "Guest" casting was done, the director would fly to the location. Meanwhile a writer would work on a second draft of the next script, getting it to us in time for our weekend polishing chores.

On one occasion, Ted, Tony Garner, and I reworked a script in my second office at the Münster barracks. We took it in turns on a word processor and batted ideas backward and forward. A real bit of team effort and good fun too. A cheery supper on completion—bratwurst and sauerkraut (Tony's favorite).

Now I must own up to the idea I had allowed to mature—about how we overcame bits of scenes or intrusive lines of dialogue we were contractually "obliged" to include in a script. The applicable director and I marked the offending section with dotted lines; he or she would then shoot the scene in full, but in such a way as the not very good part could be dropped onto the cutting room floor. As a result everyone was happy—those who had given the instruction saw everything in the rushes, and by the time the film was edited, they had forgotten all about the omitted pieces. And it did not cost us any extra shooting time!

It was wonderful to be so busy because more often than not, as I had told Holly Aird when she was still a child, there is little a producer has to do once filming has started—unless, of course, a show goes off the rails. On *Soldier, Soldier* I would be dealing with all the stages of a production simultaneously—story line, rewrites, hiring a director, casting, visiting the crew on location (didn't half clock up some air miles with my weekly trips), viewing rushes, viewing assemblies, keeping an eye on dubbing and music recording, and delivering the film to Central.

But essentially this was a gang show, expertly handled by many, many people behind the camera and by numerous in front of it—the series is rich with characters.

The plan was to go out with a bang—and on the theory that it is best not to film the last episode at the end of the schedule, when time might be running out and shortcuts could become the order of the day, we decided to do it in position number ten of the thirteen.

The draft screenplay arrived, and with the usual continuity, tweaking it would be fine—plenty of military action (with conflict!) and good personal strands. The only thing was, though, it wasn't really an end story.

"Let's make it episode twelve and find something to whet the audience's appetite for the next series," I said to David Young over a Thai lunch we hoped would be paid for from the budget.

The newspapers were currently full of the worsening situation in Bosnia and informing us that British troops were going to be sent into the war zone as part of a NATO peacekeeping force—among them the Coldstream Guards from the barracks in Münster.

Well there it was, waiting for us on a plate—our fictitious regiment would be sent there too. The last episode would simply deal with goodbyes, confessions, and reaffirmations of love and the very real fear that some of the men may never come home. Of all the scripts, this proved to be the easiest one to write. The characters' highly charged emotions spilled easily onto paper.

Central was a touch nervous about it for two reasons. First, by the time the episode was transmitted, the troubles may have been over, thus taking the wind out of the sails, or, worse, a tragedy might occur in the same week involving British soldiers, and out of respect the airing would have to have been canceled.

The risk had to be taken, and Ted had the nerve to sanction it on behalf of the company.

Tony Garner directed with great sympathy, and every one of the actors hit their performance right on the mark, not an ounce of mawkishness—realism. It was almost like a fly-on-the-wall documentary so real was it.

When I felt a sting in my eyes as we were editing the film, I knew we had got it right.

Postscript

Ted called me the day after the last episode had aired and told me the overnight ratings showed an all-time high for the series. He went on to say he had received a letter from Central TV's managing director, Leslie Hill, claiming it had been one of the best things he had ever seen on television. Apparently he too had tears in his eyes at the end.

How to beat jet lag—London to Auckland via Los Angeles, for example.

Flight departure 15:00. As soon as the aircraft is aloft, put your watch back eight hours to Pacific standard time—7:00. Have a light meal and think of it as breakfast. Take a mild sedative (possibly with a cognac for greater efficacy) and go to sleep for three hours. By then it will be around 11:00 in Los Angeles. Have another light snack—a sort of brunch—and then read a book for a few more hours. Land and enjoy a couple of evening drinks on the ground.

Reboard and set your watch forward three hours to Auckland time—by then say sometime after midnight on the day after next. Enjoy supper with a little wine, and by then you should be knackered—if not sniff a dab of essence of lavender—that'll do it. Drop into a deep sleep and wake as the sun rises on the left-hand side. Breakfast—kiwifruit.

Land fully refreshed a few hours later—still in the early part of the morning. Have a shower and get on with the day.

By applying similar techniques on the return flight, you can leave New Zealand at eight o'clock in the evening and (effectively) arrive in London the next morning—a day omitted as a result of crossing the international date line.

CHAPTER NINE

"Cut!"

There was more and more evidence that the best years of British television drama were slowly playing themselves out. Very sad, but the proliferation of TV channels was spreading the audience too thinly (six to eight million viewers in the United Kingdom is now considered good, whereas it used to be fourteen or fifteen), and fewer and fewer "risks" can be taken—where is there any excitement without risk?

In an attempt to minimize the risk factor, whole committees have to agree about a subject before it can be green-lighted—script editors "will out"! This is a totally impractical way of working. How the hell will, say, ten people make a better judgment than just one person with talent? Either could be right or could be wrong. How would a committee view something like *The Knowledge* and its group of would-be taxi drivers? "Never appeal to the Americans!"

It's a gold mining business and always will be—courage is the only essential even in the face of losing your job. Ultimately the audience alone will decide what subject matter it likes, always assuming a show is well presented in the first place. The dithering of too many so-called commissioning editors, program schedulers, and their staff is little short of catastrophic with an unacceptable number of series going into production at the eleventh hour with insufficient preparation for either script or production. The money wasting result of these makes one shudder.

What about producers? Nowadays around eight are credited on screen in various forms—coproducer, executive, associate, supervising, line, assistant. (It wouldn't surprise me if a pet dog is billed one day, or has it already been done? Maybe a question for Holly Aird!) Heaven alone knows what they all do with themselves to pass the time of day. Why are personal screen credits more important than the product?

To be absolutely fair, there is good material to be found on television, although one has to dig deeper and suffer longer waits between one nugget and the next. And computer imaging offers up many opportunities for visual enhancement, but please God, may the facility remain in the hands of storytellers and not graphic artists often too intent on playing with their tools!

Very sad news today—John Hawkesworth has died unexpectedly at the age of eighty-two on September 30, 2003. Although it is now many years since we worked together, we had always remained in contact, and Sally-Ann and I were looking forward to seeing his cheeriness and sharing a glass or two of wine with him at a sixth exhibition of his evocative paintings—barely three weeks hence as I write. There is now a void in my life where once stood a kind and thoughtful man.

Postscript

For me, after *Soldier, Soldier,* it was back with Henry Herbert (as joint producer—sadly not director) to make a cinema film I had scripted—disappointing! Even more so because it was to be the last we made together.

The news in the past week or so has been lousy; on October 7, 2003, Henry died after a long illness aged just sixty-four—that void has become wider.

But what does a chap do in the new millennium?

All my life I have wanted to be a part of musical theater working as lyricist and, if needs be, producer. When I met Ethan Lewis Maltby in the mid-1990s, I knew the time was opportune. He composes music with tunes and, still in his twenties, is a romantic—no wonder he succeeded in wooing his pretty and gifted wife, Renée Salewski, who is an up-and-coming Canadian-born opera singer.

After several years of hard work and various concert and showcase performances, our production—*Courtenay*—was finally staged for a limited run at a thousand-seat theater in full (and I mean in full—it is an enormous production and probably on a grander scale than any film or television show I have ever been involved with). What's more is it's a period drama, and I feel back where I belong.

The director was George Roman—George, who had had the essential courage to put *Monsignor Quixote* on stage—our set designer was Roy Stannard, and Malcolm Burgess was the financial director. Tony Garner even stepped around from behind the camera to return to his roots as an actor. And both Dai Bradley (*The Flame Trees of Thika*) and Julian Glover (*QED*) have appeared in the productions.

Very good reviews, but at the moment I can only say, "We'll see what happens next."

Briefly, while on the subject of reviews, can any television critic tell me why his or her role has any meaning in life? However keen, however observant, however witty, or however good a writer they may be, surely they're impotent—something like a person who hands you last week's list of special offers from Safeway.

Autumn, 2003

Jack Rosenthal—"So is that it, then?"

~

Afterword

Christopher Neame's book is a delightful read. It brought back memories of one of the most enjoyable periods of my life. Although Euston Films was owned by Thames Television, I, as chief executive, was given pretty much a free rein to make the decisions as to what drama programs we would make. We were fortunate to work with some of the most talented directors and producers. Christopher was one of these, combining the deviousness necessary to be a good producer, with dedication, optimism, charm, and a sense of humor. The book reminded me of an incident on *The Flame Trees of Thika*, which was certainly one of the most ambitious projects that Euston Films had put into production. It was fraught with difficulties: we were filming in Africa with children and animals, and we had a very tight budget. I traveled to the location with John Hawkesworth. After a horrendous journey, with no sleep, I arrived in a foul mood. Christopher met us at the airport, all smiles. "I've arranged for us to have a curry at the Muthaiga Club."

"All I want to do is go straight to bed!" I said crossly.

But he wouldn't take no for an answer. He was right, of course. I had a delicious lunch, went to sleep for twenty-four hours, and woke the next day, happy and ready for anything he had in store.

Smart move, Christopher!

—Verity Lambert

APPENDIX

~

Christopher Neame's
Films and Series for Television
(Dates of Actual Production)

Date	Film or Series Name	Title/Job
1978	*Danger UXB*	Associate producer
1979	*The Knowledge*	Producer
1980	*The Flame Trees of Thika*	Producer
1981–1982	*QED*	Producer
1983	*The Irish RM*	Producer
1985	*Monsignor Quixote*	Screenwriter and producer
1986–1987	*Bellman and True*	Producer
1991	*Bye, Bye, Baby*	Producer
1993	*Soldier, Soldier*	Producer

Index

~

About the Author

Christopher Neame's roots are firmly embedded in the film industry. The grandson of actress Ivy Close and son of director Ronald Neame, Christopher has been responsible for many film and television productions. He is currently producing a stage musical, *Courtenay*, for which he also wrote the book and lyrics. His first book, *Rungs on a Ladder: Hammer Films Seen through a Soft Gauze*, was published by Scarecrow Press in 2003.